SECRET CODES for Handhelds

2006

D0062510

A NOTE TO PARENTS

This book is an exclusive Scholastic edition that has been edited to remove all Mature-rated codes, as well as games that include excessive violence, sexual content, and inappropriate codes for children.

This book includes only E, E+, and T-rated games.

In addition, this book provides a listing of the ESRB ratings for all games included inside.

EARLY CHILDHOOD

 Titles rated EC (Early Childhood) have content that may be suitable for ages 3 and older. Contains no material that parents would find inappropriate.

EVERYONE

 Titles rated **E (Everyone)** have content that may be suitable for ages 6 and older. Titles in this category may contain minimal cartoon, fantasy or mild violence and/or infrequent use of mild language.

EVERYONE 10+

 Titles rated **E10+ (Everyone 10 and older)** have content that may be suitable for ages 10 and older. Titles in this category may contain more cartoon, fantasy or mild violence, mild language, and/or minimal suggestive themes.

TEEN

 Titles rated **T (Teen)** have content that may be suitable for ages 13 and older. Titles in this category may contain violence, suggestive themes, crude humor, minimal blood and/or infrequent use of strong language.

MATURE

 Titles rated **M (Mature)** have content that may be suitable for persons ages 17 and older. Titles in this category may contain intense violence, blood and gore, sexual content, and/or strong language.

ADULTS ONLY

 Titles rated **AO (Adults Only)** have content that should only be played by persons 18 years and older. Titles in this category may include prolonged scenes of intense violence and/or graphic sexual content and nudity.

Everyone

ACE COMBAT ADVANCE

ACTION MAN: ROBOT ATAK

ALIENATORS: EVOLUTION CONTINUES

ANIMAL SNAP: RESCUE THEM 2 BY 2

AROUND THE WORLD IN 80 DAYS

BACKYARD BASEBALL 2006

BANJO PILOT

BEYBLADE: ULTIMATE BLADER JAM

BIONICLE: TALES OF THE TOHUNGA

BOXING FEVER

BUBBLE BOBBLE OLD AND NEW

BUTT UGLY MARTIANS: B.K.M. BATTLES

CAR BATTLER JOE

CARTOON NETWORK SPEEDWAY

DANNY PHANTOM: THE ULTIMATE ENEMY

DISNEY'S EXTREME SKATE ADVENTURE

DISNEY'S HOME ON THE RANGE

DK: KING OF SWING

DONKEY KONG COUNTRY 2: DIDDY KONG'S QUEST

DORA THE EXPLORER: SUPER SPIES

FINAL FANTASY I & II: DAWN OF SOULS

GT ADVANCE 3: PRO CONCEPT RACING

HOT WHEELS VELOCITY X

ICE AGE

THE INCREDIBLES

IRIDION II

Everyone (continued)

JUSTICE LEAGUE: INJUSTICE FOR ALL

KIEN

LEGO KNIGHT'S KINGDOM

LEGO STAR WARS

MEGA MAN BATTLE NETWORK 5: TEAM PROTOMAN

MEGA MAN BATTLE NETWORK 5: TEAM COLONEL

MONSTER FORCE

NICKTOONS UNITE!

ROAD TRIP: SHIFTING GEARS

RUGRATS: I GOTTA GO PARTY

SECRET AGENT BARBIE: ROYAL JEWELS MISSION

SEGA SMASH PACK

SHAMAN KING: LEGACY OF THE SPIRITS, SOARING HAWK

SHAMAN KING: LEGACY OF THE SPIRITS, SPRINTING WOLF

SHINING SOUL

SHINING SOUL II

SPIDER-MAN 2

SPYRO ORANGE: THE CORTEX CONSPIRACY

SUPER MONKEY BALL JR

SUPER PUZZLE FIGHTER 2 TURBO

THAT'S SO RAVEN 2: SUPERNATURAL STYLE

TOM AND JERRY: THE MAGIC RING

TONY HAWK'S UNDERGROUND

TONY HAWK'S UNDERGROUND 2

TOP GUN: COMBAT ZONES

TRON 2.0: KILLER APP

THE URBZ: SIMS IN THE CITY

WINNIE THE POOH'S RUMBLY TUMBLY ADVENTURE

WORLD CHAMPIONSHIP POKER

XXX

YOSHI TOPSY-TURVY

YU-GI-OH! 7 TRIALS TO GLORY: WORLD CHAMPIONSHIP TOURNAMENT 2005

YU-GI-OH! DESTINY BOARD TRAVELER

ZOIDS: LEGACY

E 10+

DRAGON BALL GT: TRANSFORMATION

POWER RANGERS: SPACE PATROL DELTA

Teen

BLACKTHORNE

BLADES OF THUNDER

BUFFY THE VAMPIRE SLAYER: WRATH OF THE DARKHUL KING

CASTLEVANIA: ARIA OF SORROW

CT SPECIAL FORCES 3: NAVY OPS

RIVER CITY RANSOM EX

ROAD RASH: JAILBREAK

STREET FIGHTER ALPHA 3

TOMB RAIDER: THE PROPHECY

URBAN YETI

GAME BOY® ADVANCE

Game Boy® Advance Table of Contents:

ACE COMBAT ADVANCE

COMPLETE GAME WITH ALL PLANES AND LEVELS OPEN

Select Enter Code and enter **QF9B9F59**.

ACTION MAN: ROBOT ATAK

ADVENTURE LEVEL 2
Select Password from the main menu and enter **REDWOLF**.

ADVENTURE LEVEL 3
Select Password from the main menu and enter **FLYNT**.

ADVENTURE LEVEL 4
Select Password from the main menu and enter **MOTHER**.

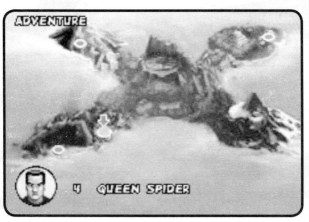

ADVENTURE LEVEL 5
Select Password from the main menu and enter **MOTOX**.

ADVENTURE LEVEL 6
Select Password from the main menu and enter **TEMPLE**.

ADVENTURE LEVEL 7
Select Password from the main menu and enter **ACTION**.

ADVENTURE LEVEL 8
Select Password from the main menu and enter **BEACH**.

ADVENTURE LEVEL 9
Select Password from the main menu and enter **JURA**.

ADVENTURE LEVEL 10
Select Password from the main menu and enter **AIR**.

ADVENTURE LEVEL 11
Select Password from the main menu and enter **SURF**.

ADVENTURE LEVEL 12
Select Password from the main menu and enter **SEWERS**.

ADVENTURE LEVEL 13
Select Password from the main menu and enter **TUNNEL**.

ADVENTURE LEVEL 14
Select Password from the main menu and enter **LABO**.

ADVENTURE LEVEL 15
Select Password from the main menu and enter **KONGO**.

ADVENTURE LEVEL 16
Select Password from the main menu and enter **BASIC**.

ADVENTURE LEVEL 17
Select Password from the main menu and enter **ROCKET**.

ADVANCED MODE
Select Password from the main menu and enter **JUNGLE**.

ADVANCED LEVEL 2
Select Password from the main menu and enter **AZTEC**.

ADVANCED LEVEL 3
Select Password from the main menu and enter **SPIDER**.

ADVANCED LEVEL 4
Select Password from the main menu and enter **DIRT**.

ADVANCED LEVEL 5
Select Password from the main menu and enter **CROCO**.

ADVANCED LEVEL 6
Select Password from the main menu and enter **QUEEN**.

ADVANCED LEVEL 7
Select Password from the main menu and enter **BOW**.

ADVANCED LEVEL 8
Select Password from the main menu and enter **LAVA**.

ADVANCED LEVEL 9
Select Password from the main menu and enter **ROCKS**.

ADVANCED LEVEL 10
Select Password from the main menu and enter **VOLCANO**.

ADVANCED LEVEL 11
Select Password from the main menu and enter **TRAPS**.

ADVANCED LEVEL 12
Select Password from the main menu and enter **DINO**.

ADVANCED LEVEL 13
Select Password from the main menu and enter **SHORE**.

ADVANCED LEVEL 14
Select Password from the main menu and enter **RAPTOR**.

ADVANCED LEVEL 15
Select Password from the main menu and enter **BATS**.

ADVANCED LEVEL 16
Select Password from the main menu and enter **TREX**.

ADVANCED LEVEL 17
Select Password from the main menu and enter **BIRD**.

ADVANCED LEVEL 18
Select Password from the main menu and enter **ATTACK**.

ADVANCED LEVEL 19
Select Password from the main menu and enter **SHELL**.

ADVANCED LEVEL 20
Select Password from the main menu and enter **PATROL**.

ADVANCED LEVEL 21
Select Password from the main menu and enter **WIND**.

ADVANCED LEVEL 22
Select Password from the main menu and enter **RATS**.

ADVANCED LEVEL 23
Select Password from the main menu and enter **SECRET**.

ADVANCED LEVEL 24
Select Password from the main menu and enter **WATER**.

ADVANCED LEVEL 25
Select Password from the main menu and enter **VAPOR**.

ADVANCED LEVEL 26
Select Password from the main menu and enter **MORAN**.

ADVANCED LEVEL 27
Select Password from the main menu and enter **LIANA**.

ADVANCED LEVEL 28
Select Password from the main menu and enter **BACK**.

ADVANCED LEVEL 29
Select Password from the main menu and enter **CLOCK**.

ADVANCED LEVEL 30
Select Password from the main menu and enter **UNITY**.

ADVANCED LEVEL 31
Select Password from the main menu and enter **FINAL**.

ADVANCED LEVEL 32
Select Password from the main menu and enter **DOCTORX**.

TIME ATTACK MODE
Select Password from the main menu and enter **HURRY**.

TIME ATTACK 2
Select Password from the main menu and enter **RUINS**.

TIME ATTACK MODE IS REALLY SIMPLE:

COMPLETE THE LEVEL BEFORE THE
CLOCK COUNTS DOWN TO 0!

TIME ATTACK 3
Select Password from the main menu and enter **VENOM**.

TIME ATTACK 4
Select Password from the main menu and enter **STORM**.

TIME ATTACK 5
Select Password from the main menu and enter **BAYOU**.

TIME ATTACK 6
Select Password from the main menu and enter **EGGS**.

TIME ATTACK 7
Select Password from the main menu and enter **ARROW**.

TIME ATTACK 8
Select Password from the main menu and enter **RACE**.

TIME ATTACK 9
Select Password from the main menu and enter **SLOPE**.

9   SHOOTING ROCKS

TIME ATTACK 10
Select Password from the main menu and enter **HASTE**.

TIME ATTACK 11
Select Password from the main menu and enter **PITFALL**.

TIME ATTACK 12
Select Password from the main menu and enter **DESCENT**.

TIME ATTACK 13
Select Password from the main menu and enter **RUN**.

TIME ATTACK 14
Select Password from the main menu and enter **CLAWS**.

TIME ATTACK 15
Select Password from the main menu and enter **STONES**.

TIME ATTACK 16
Select Password from the main menu and enter **WAOW**.

TIME ATTACK 17
Select Password from the main menu and enter **AERO**.

TIME ATTACK 18
Select Password from the main menu and enter **BREEZE**.

TIME ATTACK 19
Select Password from the main menu and enter **RUSH**.

TIME ATTACK 20
Select Password from the main menu and enter **CLOUDS**.

TIME ATTACK 21
Select Password from the main menu and enter **GUST**.

TIME ATTACK 22
Select Password from the main menu and enter **STINK**.

TIME ATTACK 23
Select Password from the main menu and enter **BASE**.

TIME ATTACK 24
Select Password from the main menu and enter **DANGER**.

TIME ATTACK 25
Select Password from the main menu and enter **STEAM**.

TIME ATTACK 26
Select Password from the main menu and enter **RESCUE**.

TIME ATTACK 27
Select Password from the main menu and enter **MONKEY**.

TIME ATTACK 28
Select Password from the main menu and enter **CHAMBER**.

TIME ATTACK 29
Select Password from the main menu and enter **BANANA**.

TIME ATTACK 30
Select Password from the main menu and enter **FORCE**.

TIME ATTACK 31
Select Password from the main menu and enter **TELE**.

TIME ATTACK 32

Select Password from the main menu and enter **BOSS**.

GAME COMPLETE

Select Password from the main menu and enter **MAXIM**.

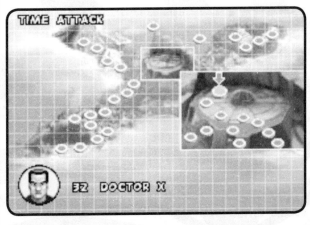

ALIENATORS: EVOLUTION CONTINUES

LEVEL 2
Enter **MDKMZKCC** as a password.

LEVEL 3
Enter **BHSZSKTC** as a password.

LEVEL 4
Enter **ZKTSHKMC** as a password.

LEVEL 5
Enter **JLPFDKHB** as a password.

LEVEL 6
Enter **HMDBRKCB** as a password.

LEVEL 7
Enter **GLDKLKZB** as a password.

LEVEL 8
Enter **GLPKLKRB** as a password.

LEVEL 9
Enter **GLDJBKKF** as a password.

LEVEL 10
Enter **GLPJBKFF** as a password.

LEVEL 11
Enter **GLPKBKRF** as a password.

LEVEL 12
Enter **GLPKBKRF** as a password.

LEVEL 13
Enter **GLDJLKHD** as a password.

UNLIMITED AMMO
Enter RBJPXCKC as a password.

ANIMAL SNAP: RESCUE THEM 2 BY 2

BLOCK BLASTER MINI-GAME
At the main menu, hold L and press Up, Down, Left, Right, Right, Left, Down, Up.

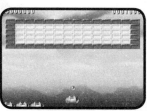

AROUND THE WORLD IN 80 DAYS

PASSWORDS

LEVEL	PASSWORD
Day 1 - London	BHGG
Day 3 - Paris	CLGG
Day 18 - Train	DCHJ
Day 20 - Turkey	FSHJ
Day 25 - India	GKMN
Day 25 - Wanted in India	HLSN
Day 40 - China	JMBJ
Day 61 - San Francisco	KNQN
Day 61 - Train to New York	MQGG
Day 61 - Wild West	LPGG
Old Foe	NRGG
Ending	PSGG

BEYBLADE: ULTIMATE BLADER JAM

ALL BEYBLADES

At the Title screen, press B, L, R, Down.

DESTROY ENEMIES
Pause the game and press Up, Up, Right, Left, L.

BIT BEAST ATTACK METER
Pause the game and press Right, Left, Right, Left.

BLACKTHORNE

INFINITE HEALTH
At the title screen, press Left, Right, Down, Up, B, B, Down.

INVISIBLE
At the title screen, press B, Down, Right, Down, Up, Up, Left, B, Up.

FALLING WON'T KILL YOU
At the title screen, press B, B, Up, Left, Down, Right, Right, Up.

BOXING FEVER

PASSWORDS

COMPLETE	PASSWORD
Amateur Series	90HG6738
Top Contender Series	H7649DH5
Pro Am Series	2GG48HD9
Professional Series	8G3D97B7
World Title	B3G58318
Survival Mode	G51FF888

BUBBLE BOBBLE OLD AND NEW

BUBBLE BOBBLE NEW: SUPER MODE

At the Bubble Bobble New Title screen, press Right, R, Left, L, Select, R, Select, L.

BUBBLE BOBBLE OLD: ORIGINAL MODE

At the Bubble Bobble Old Title screen, press L, R, L, R, L, R, Right, Select.

BUBBLE BOBBLE OLD: POWER-UP MODE

At the Bubble Bobble Old Title screen, press Select, R, L, Left, Right, R, Select, Right.

BUBBLE BOBBLE OLD: SUPER MODE

At the Bubble Bobble Old Title screen, press Left, R, Left, Select, Left, L, Left, Select.

BLADES OF THUNDER

LEVEL 1 ON EASY

Enter the password **4265**.

LEVEL 2 ON EASY

Enter the password **7332**.

LEVEL 3 ON EASY
Enter the password **6578**.

LEVEL 4 ON EASY
Enter the password **7213**.

LEVEL 5 ON EASY
Enter the password **8234**.

LEVEL 6 ON EASY
Enter the password **9322**.

LEVEL 7 ON EASY
Enter the password **1279**.

LEVEL 8 ON EASY
Enter the password **5682**.

LEVEL 9 ON EASY
Enter the password **3211**.

LEVEL 1 ON MEDIUM
Enter the password **6932**.

LEVEL 2 ON MEDIUM
Enter the password **3682**.

LEVEL 3 ON MEDIUM
Enter the password **5892**.

LEVEL 4 ON MEDIUM
Enter the password **4468**.

LEVEL 5 ON MEDIUM
Enter the password **1127**.

LEVEL 6 ON MEDIUM
Enter the password **9902**.

LEVEL 7 ON MEDIUM
Enter the password **2332**.

LEVEL 8 ON MEDIUM
Enter the password **8658**.

LEVEL 9 ON MEDIUM
Enter the password **7745**.

LEVEL 1 ON HARD
Enter the password **1979**.

LEVEL 2 ON HARD
Enter the password **2034**.

LEVEL 3 ON HARD
Enter the password **7809**.

LEVEL 4 ON HARD
Enter the password **6776**.

LEVEL 5 ON HARD
Enter the password **9054**.

LEVEL 6 ON HARD
Enter the password **4311**.

LEVEL 7 ON HARD
Enter the password **8282**.

LEVEL 8 ON HARD
Enter the password **2468**.

LEVEL 9 ON HARD
Enter the password **1410**.

BUFFY THE VAMPIRE SLAYER: WRATH OF THE DARKHUL KING

9 OF EVERYTHING
At the title screen, press Up, Down, Up, Down, B, A.

INFINITE LIVES
At the title screen, press L, L, L, R, R, R, Right, Right.

INVINCIBLE
At the title screen, press B, B, A, A, L, R, Down, Up.

BUTT UGLY MARTIANS: B.K.M. BATTLES

UNLIMITED LIVES
Enter **KMIORMAO** as a password.

MAX DEFENSE, FIREPOWER AND RESTORATION PICKUPS
Enter **ALWMAA15** as a password.

2 DEFENSE UPGRADES
Enter **JT2DU 4MP** as a password.

2 EXTRA LIVES
Enter **2ELFM PLS** as a password.

2 WEAPON UPGRADES
Enter **GMACO EWU** as a password.

4 DEFENSE UPGRADES
Enter **DUATO U4M** as a password.

4 EXTRA LIVES
Enter **IAGAW 4EL** as a password.

4 WEAPON UPGRADES
Enter **IAGAW 4WU** as a password.

START AT MECHTROPOLIS
Select Resume Game and enter **IWTSOWN2**.

START AT AQUATICA
Select Resume Game and enter **TMTWN3PD**.

START AT ARBOREA
Select Resume Game and enter **IIALTSMO4**.

START AT SILICON CITY
Select Resume Game and enter **IOTJOWN5**.

START AT MAGMA
Select Resume Game and enter **FILGSOW6**.

START AT KOO FOO SHIP
Select Resume Game and enter **IWTSOWN7**.

CAR BATTLER JOE

BIG BANG

At the main menu, select Battle League. When the game asks "Use which machine," choose password and enter **HAMA!333**.

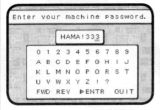

BLUE GALPE EV

At the main menu, select Battle League. When the game asks "Use which machine," choose password and enter **SHISYO!!**.

CASEY'S WHLS

At the main menu, select Battle League. When the game asks "Use which machine," choose password and enter **!KOKICHI**.

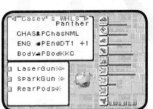

CAVALIER

At the main menu, select Battle League. When the game asks "Use which machine," choose password and enter **CUREWAND**.

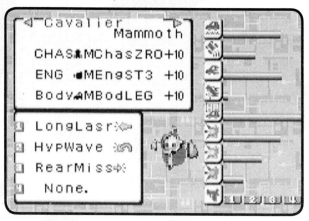

COPA ZONE23

At the main menu, select Battle League. When the game asks "Use which machine," choose password and enter **CDMACAPA**.

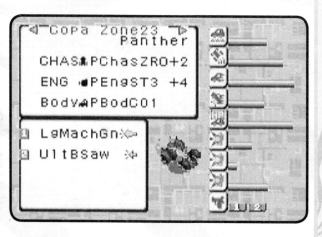

EMP FORCE X

At the main menu, select Battle League. When the game asks "Use which machine," choose password and enter **EMPIRE!!**.

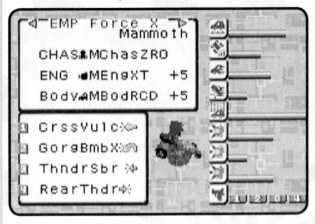

ISSUE X

At the main menu, select Battle League. When the game asks "Use which machine," choose password and enter **8998981!**.

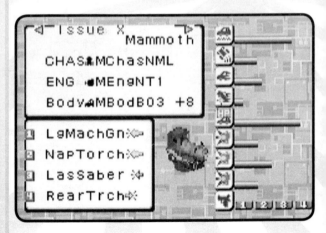

JOE JIM ZERO

At the main menu, select Battle League. When the game asks "Use which machine," choose password and enter Todoroki.

LONG VALLEYZ

At the main menu, select Battle League. When the game asks "Use which machine," choose password and enter **NAGOYADB**.

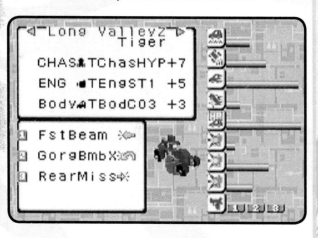

MATSU K MK4

At the main menu, select Battle League. When the game asks "Use which machine," choose password and enter **MR!HURRY**.

MAX-K

At the main menu, select Battle League. When the game asks "Use which machine," choose password and enter **GANKOMAX**.

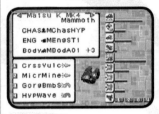
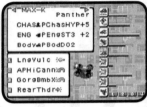

MEGA M

At the main menu, select Battle League. When the game asks "Use which machine," choose password and enter **M!M!M!M!**.

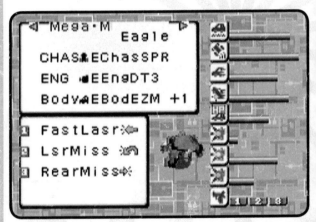

MILLENNIUM90

At the main menu, select Battle League. When the game asks "Use which machine," choose password and enter **90!60!92**.

MRIN'S DREAM

At the main menu, select Battle League. When the game asks "Use which machine," choose password and enter **MARRON!!**.

MSSL DOLLY

At the main menu, select Battle League. When the game asks "Use which machine," choose password and enter **KINNIKU!**.

PISTON GH

At the main menu, select Battle League. When the game asks "Use which machine," choose password and enter **GO!HOME!**.

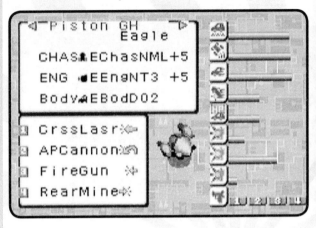

SOLID WIND

At the main menu, select Battle League. When the game asks "Use which machine," choose password and enter **RED!GUNS**.

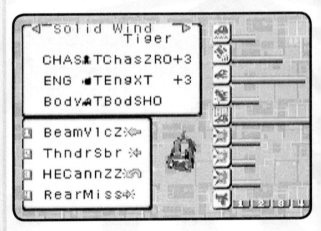

TAKAH'S LSR

At the main menu, select Battle League. When the game asks "Use which machine," choose password and enter **TK000056**.

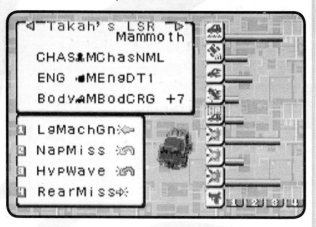

WNN SPECIAL

At the main menu, select Battle League. When the game asks "Use which machine," choose password and enter **BOM!BOM!**.

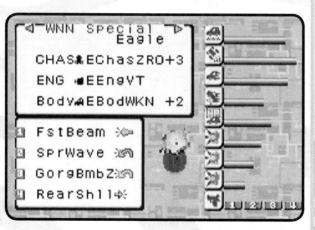

CARTOON NETWORK SPEEDWAY

UNLOCK EVERYTHING
Enter **96981951** as a password.

ALL FIVE CHAMPIONSHIPS COMPLETE
Enter **34711154** as a password.

START AT FARM FROLICS
Enter **12761357** as a password.

START AT DOWN ON THE FARM
Enter **25731079** as a password.

START AT MURIEL
Enter **25731079** as a password.

START AT EDOPOLIS
Enter **38611791** as a password.

START AT JOHNNY 2X4
Enter **52681314** as a password.

START AT SCARY SPEEDWAY
Enter **68851752** as a password.

START AT DESERT DRIVE
Enter **81821475** as a password.

START AT LITTLE SUZY
Enter **81821475** as a password.

START AT HOT ROD JOHNNY
Enter **84891097** as a password.

START AT SWANKY
Enter **98761719** as a password.

START AT ALPINE ANTICS
Enter **98761719** as a password.

ACME AXEL AWARD TROPHY
Enter **50000050** as a password.

CARTOON SPEEDWAY TROPHY
Enter **10000010** as a password.

FENDER BENDER FRENZY TROPHY
Enter **32000010** as a password.

CASTLEVANIA: ARIA OF SORROW

NO ITEMS

Start a new game with the name **NOUSE** to use no items in the game.

NO SOULS

Start a new game with the name **NOSOUL** to use no souls in the game.

CT SPECIAL FORCES 3: NAVY OPS

LEVEL 1-2

Enter **5073** as a password.

LEVEL 2-1

Enter **1427** as a password.

LEVEL 2-2

Enter **2438** as a password.

LEVEL 2-3

Enter **7961** as a password.

LEVEL 2-4

Enter **8721** as a password.

LEVEL 3-1

Enter **5986** as a password.

LEVEL 3-2

Enter **2157** as a password.

LEVEL 3-3

Enter **4796** as a password.

LEVEL 3-4

Enter **3496** as a password.

LEVEL 3-5

Enter **1592** as a password.

LEVEL 3-6

Enter **4168** as a password.

LEVEL 3-7

Enter **1364** as a password.

LEVEL 4-1

Enter **7596** as a password.

LEVEL 4-2
Enter **9108** as a password.

LEVEL 4-3
Enter **6124** as a password.

LEVEL 4-4
Enter **7234** as a password.

LEVEL 4-5
Enter **6820** as a password.

LEVEL 5-1
Enter **2394** as a password.

LEVEL 5-2
Enter **4256** as a password.

LEVEL 5-3
Enter **0842** as a password.

DANNY PHANTOM: THE ULTIMATE ENEMY

BOSS RUSH MODE
Select Password from the Options and enter **Rush**.

EASY AND HARD DIFFICULTY
Select Password from the Options and enter **Vlad**.

DASH'S HAUNTED LOCKER MINI GAME
Select Password from the Options and enter **Dash**.

HINDIN' GHOST SEEK MINI GAME
Select Password from the Options and enter **Seek**.

LEVITATION MINI GAME
Select Password from the Options and enter **Jazz**.

SAM'S X-RAY ECTO DETECTOR MINI GAME
Select Password from the Options and enter **Ecto**.

DISNEY'S EXTREME SKATE ADVENTURE

PETER PAN
At the main menu, press L, R, L, R, L, L, **START**.

DISNEY'S HOME ON THE RANGE

LEVEL 1
Enter **DVHB** as a password.

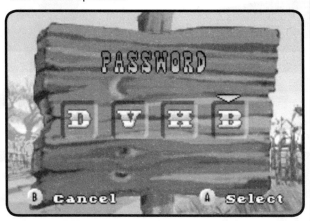

LEVEL 2
Enter **VCFK** as a password.

LEVEL 3
Enter **BQMF** as a password.

LEVEL 4
Enter **HFKM** as a password.

LEVEL 5
Enter **DMCV** as a password.

LEVEL 6
Enter **BBKD** as a password.

LEVEL 7
Enter **KNLC** as a password.

LEVEL 8
Enter **BDJR** as a password.

LEVEL 9
Enter **BDRN** as a password.

LEVEL 10
Enter **PSBH** as a password.

LEVEL 11
Enter **QRNN** as a password.

LEVEL 12
Enter **MMKN** as a password.

LEVEL 13
Enter **PSFH** as a password.

LEVEL 14
Enter **DBVJ** as a password.

DK: KING OF SWING

ATTACK BATTLE 3
At the title screen, press Up + L + A + B to bring up a password screen. Enter **65942922**.

CLIMBING RACE 5
At the title screen, press Up + L + A + B to bring up a password screen. Enter **55860327**.

OBSTACLE RACE 4
At the title screen, press Up + L + A + B to bring up a password screen. Enter **35805225**.

UNLOCK TIME ATTACK
Complete the game as DK.

UNLOCK DIDDY MODE
Collect 24 medals as DK.

UNLOCK BUBBLES
Complete Diddy Mode with 24 Medals.

UNLOCK KREMLING
Collect 6 gold medals in Jungle Jam.

UNLOCK KING K. ROOL
Collect 12 gold medals in Jungle Jam.

DONKEY KONG COUNTRY 2: DIDDY KONG'S QUEST

ALL LEVELS

Select Cheats from the Options and enter freedom.

START WITH 15 LIVES

Select Cheats from the Options and enter **helpme**.

START WITH 55 LIVES

Select Cheats from the Options and enter **weakling**.

START WITH 10 BANANA COINS

Select Cheats from the Options and enter **richman**.

START WITH 50 BANANA COINS

Select Cheats from the Options and enter **wellrich**.

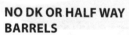

NO DK OR HALF WAY BARRELS

Select Cheats from the Options and enter **rockard**.

MUSIC PLAYER
Select Cheats from the Options and enter **onetime**.

CREDITS
Select Cheats from the Options and enter **kredits**.

DORA THE EXPLORER: SUPER SPIES

RAINFOREST 2 PASSWORD
Select Continue and enter Arrow up, Plus sign, Triangle, Star, Plus sign, Triangle, Frown.

DRAGON BALL GT: TRANSFORMATION

REFILL ENERGY
During a game, press Down, Up, Right. Right, Right, Left, Right, Left, B.

REFILL HEALTH
During a game, press Down, Up, Left, Left, Up, Right, Down, B.

PICCOLO
At the main menu, press Left, Right, Left Right, Up, Up, Down, B.

SUPER BABY VEGETA
At the main menu, press Left, Right, Left Right, Down, Down, Up, B.

SUPER SAIYAN 4 GOKU
At the main menu, press Left, Right, Left Right, Down, Down, Down, B.

SUPER SAIYAN KID GOKU
At the main menu, press Left, Right, Left Right, Up, Up, Up, B.

SUPER SAIYAN VEGETA
At the main menu, press Left, Right, Left Right, Up, Down, Down, B.

FINAL FANTASY I & II: DAWN OF SOULS

FF I TILE GAME
During a game of Final Fantasy I and after you get the ship, hold A and press B about 55 times.

FF II CONCENTRATION GAME
Once you obtain the Snowcraft, hold B and press A about 20 times.

GT ADVANCE 3: PRO CONCEPT RACING

ALL CARS
At the Title screen, hold L + B and press Left.

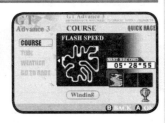

ALL TRACKS
At the Title screen, hold L + B and press Right.

ALL TUNE UPS
At the Title screen, hold L + B and press Up.

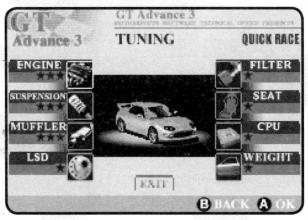

EXTRA MODES

At the Title screen, hold L + B and press Down.

HOT WHEELS VELOCITY X

PASSWORDS

LEVEL	PASSWORD	LEVEL	PASSWORD
02	143-24-813	21	766-46-341
03	141-38-985	22	187-98-394
04	249-48-723	23	188-12-234
05	294-16-277	24	786-84-747
06	457-51-438	25	466-59-979
07	112-86-545	26	477-58-369
08	447-65-112	27	447-62-191
09	368-54-466	28	614-81-432
10	718-59-438	29	641-18-239
11	363-95-545	30	399-68-584
12	373-65-848	31	662-84-635
13	171-49-211	32	476-63-843
14	373-59-216	33	616-67-341
15	373-62-927	34	384-97-475
16	718-42-276	35	363-13-298
17	358-59-355	36	521-71-135
18	478-68-254	37	543-17-658
19	573-77-683	38	782-57-387
20	188-58-352		

ICE AGE

LEVEL SELECT
Enter **NTTTTT** as a password.

ART GALLERY
Enter **MFKRPH** as a password.

LEVEL PASSWORDS

LEVEL	PASSWORD
2	PBBQBB
3	QBCQBB
4	SBFQBB
5	DBKQBB
6	NBTQBB
7	PCTQBB
8	RFTQBB
9	CKTQBB
10	MTTQBB

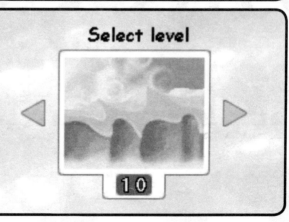

THE INCREDIBLES

PASSWORDS

LEVEL	PASSWORD
1-1-1	MSW5
1-1-2	BK8V
1-2-1	69NN
1-3-1	GFVY
1-3-2	V34K
2-1-1	94HR
2-1-2	ZWLG
2-1-3	SP??
2-2-1	KDY3
2-3-1	Y27F
2-3-2	6!2N
2-3-3	BHBV
2-4-1	MQR5
2-4-2	3YTK
2-4-3	?6DS
2-5-2	6?SR
2-5-3	SNJ5
3-1-1	MNW9
3-2-1	BF8Z
3-2-2	65NS
3-2-3	YVKK
3-2-4	KGTY
3-3-1	SDR6
3-4-1	Z3ZB
3-5-1	9?5M
3-5-2	FC73
3-5-3	NL2?
3-6-1	VXBG
3-6-2	YWKJ
3-6-3	GJQZ
3-7-1	KHP2
3-7-2	313K
4-1-1	?!JT
4-2-1	ML17

LEVEL	PASSWORD
4-3-1	YXFC
4-4-1	GHV1
4-5-1	VW4C
4-6-1	YX!F

IRIDION II

EASY PASSWORDS

LEVEL	PASSWORD
2	SBJS5
3	9CRT5
4	T3KG3
5	93PNV
6	95FN3
7	5MYCX
8	6C3L5
9	PW3NX
10	649QV
11	NFK2V
12	5DS2V
13	!GDV5
14	T7H8X
15	!9ROX
End	4RC8!

JUKEBOX

Enter **CH4LL** as a password.

JUSTICE LEAGUE: INJUSTICE FOR ALL

CAN'T BE HIT

Pause the game, press Select and unpause.

KIEN

QUEST II
Enter **KA10LVQ1M** as a password.

QUEST III
Enter **KB18LVQ2L** as a password.

QUEST IV
Enter **KC30LVQ3G** as a password.

QUEST V
Enter **KD70LVQ4S** as a password.

LEGO KNIGHT'S KINGDOM

STORY 100% COMPLETE
Enter **YZZVZYZ** as a password.

LEGO STAR WARS

SHEEP MODE
Pause the game and press L, R, L, Down, Up, R, R, Right, Left, Down, Right, Right, Select.

YODA SAYS
Pause the game and press Down, L, R, Select.

WATCH CUTSCENES
Pause the game and press Down, Up, R, L, R, R, R, Down, Down, Up, Down, Down, Select.

REPAIR BOT
Pause the game and press Down, Down, Down, Down, L, Right, Down, Right, L.

TEMPORARY SPEED BOOST
Pause the game and press Right, Right, Down, Up, Right, L.

PLAY AS BATTLE DROID
On the start screen, press **START**, **START**, Left, Down, Down, Down, Down, Right.

PLAY AS A DROIDEKA
Pause the game and press **START**, **START**, Down, Right, Left, Down, Right, Left.

PLAY AS A REPAIR DROID

Pause the game and press **START**, **START**, Up, Up, Up, Down, Down, Down.

PLAY AS BLUE GUNGAN

Pause the game and press **START**, **START**, Down, Left, Right, Down, Left, Right.

PLAY AS C-3PO

Pause the game and press press **START**, **START**, Left, Down, Right, Up, Right, Right.

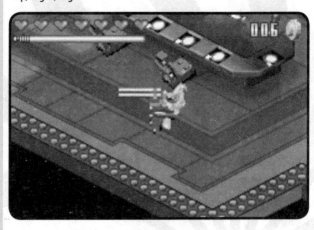

PLAY AS DROID ON HOVERSLED

Pause the game and press **START**, **START**, Down, Up, Down, Up, Down, Up.

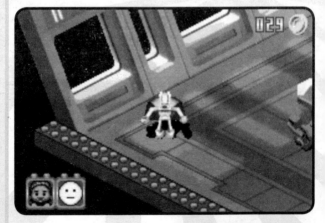

PLAY AS GENERAL GRIEVOUS

Pause the game and press **START**, **START**, Down, Down, Down, Down, Down, Down.

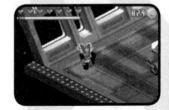

PLAY AS WINGED GUY

Pause the game and press **START**, **START**, Right, Down, Right, Down, Left, Up.

PLAY AS R2-D2

Pause the game and press **START**, **START**, Up, Up, Up, Up, Up, Up.

PLAY AS R4-P17

Pause the game and press **START**, **START**, Up, Down, Up, Down, Up, Down.

POWERFUL BLASTERS

Pause the game and press Down, Down, Left, Right, Down, L.

A FEW LEGO PIECES

Pause the game and press L, L, L, Right, Left, R, R, R.

BLACK SABER

Pause the game and press L, L, R, **START**.

BLUE SABER

Pause the game and press R, R, R, **START**.

GREEN SABER

Pause the game and press R, L, R, **START**.

PURPLE SABER

Pause the game and press L, R, L, **START**.

RED SABER

Pause the game and press L, R, R, **START**.

YELLOW SABER

Pause the game and press R, R, L, **START**.

MEGA MAN BATTLE NETWORK 5: TEAM PROTOMAN & MEGA MAN BATTLE NETWORK 5: TEAM COLONEL

To compress the following Navi Customizer Programs, you must highlight that program and enter the appropriate code.

COMPRESS AIRSHOES

Highlight AirShoes, hold Right and press B, L, B, A, B, L, B, B, A, A.

COMPRESS ATTACKMAX

Highlight AttackMAX, hold Right and press L, L, L, R, R, B, A, R, B, L.

COMPRESS BATTERYMODE

Highlight BatteryMode, hold Right and press A, A, B, R, A, B, R, L, L, R.

COMPRESS BEATSUPPORT

Highlight BeatSupport, hold Right and press A, B, B, R, A, A, B, R, B, R.

COMPRESS BODYPACK

Highlight BodyPack, hold Right and press B, A, R, A, B, R, L, R, R, A.

COMPRESS BUGSTOPPER

Highlight bugstopper, hold Right and press B, A, B, L, A, B, R, L, R, B.

COMPRESS BUSTERPACK

Highlight BusterPack, hold Right and press L, L, R, A, R, L, B, L, A, R.

COMPRESS CHARGEMAX

Highlight ChargeMAX, hold Right and press A, L, A, A, R, B, R, B, A, R.

COMPRESS COLLECT

Highlight Collect, hold Right and press B, R, A, L, A, R, B, A, A, B.

COMPRESS CUSTOM +1

Highlight , hold Right and press A, A, R, L, B, A, B, A, L, B.

COMPRESS CUSTOM2

Highlight Custom, hold Right and press B, A, R, L, L, R, A, L, B, R.

COMPRESS DANDYISM

Highlight Dandyism, hold Right and press R, R, B, B, R, B, R, B, A, A.

COMPRESS FIRST BARRIER

Highlight Barrier, hold Right and press R, L, A, B, B, A, R, A, L, R.

COMPRESS FLOATSHOES

Highlight FloatShoes, hold Right and press A, L, L, B, R, L, A, A, A, L.

COMPRESS GIGAFOLDER1

Highlight GigaFolder, hold Right and press R, R, L, B, L, L, A, R, B, L.

COMPRESS GIGAVIRUS

Highlight GigaVirus, hold Right and press B, B, R, A, L, B, L, A, R, R.

COMPRESS HUMOURSENSE

Highlight HumourSense, hold Right and press A, B, L, A, R, A, B, L, R, L.

COMPRESS I'M FISH

Highlight I'm Fish, hold Right and press B, A, B, A, L, R, A, R, A, A.

COMPRESS THE JUNGLELAND

Highlight JungleLand, hold Right and press L, R, L, A, B, L, B, B, L, A.

COMPRESS KAWARIMIMAGIC

Highlight KawarimiMagic, hold Right and press R, B, B, A, R, B, R, A, R, B.

COMPRESS MEGAFOLDER 1

Highlight , hold Right and press B, B, A, B, B, R, R, L, A, R.

COMPRESS MEGAVIRUS

Highlight MegaVirus, hold Right and press A, A, B, L, A, R, B, L, A, A.

COMPRESS MILLIONARE

Highlight Millionare, hold Right and press R, L, R, A, R, R, L, L, L, R.

COMPRESS THE OIL BODY

Highlight Oil Body, hold Right and press L, B, R, A, R, L, A, B, L, B.

COMPRESS RAPIDMAX

Highlight RapidMAX, hold Right and press R, A, R, L, L, R, R, A, B, A.

COMPRESS THE REFLECT PROGRAM

Highlight program, hold Right and press L, L, R, B, L, L, A, A, L, B.

COMPRESS RUSHSUPPORT

Highlight RushSupport, hold Right and press R, B, L, R, B, R, L, L, R, L.

COMPRESS SAITOBATCH

Highlight SaitoBatch, hold Right and press A, L, R, A, B, L, R, A, L, R.

COMPRESS SELFRECOVERY

Highlight SelfRecovery, hold Right and press R, L, R, L, R, B, B, R, A, B.

COMPRESS SHIELD

Highlight Shield, hold Right and press A, B, A, R, A, L, R, B, B, A.

COMPRESS SHINOBIDASH

Highlight ShinobiDash, hold Right and press R, L, L, A, L, L, B, A, B, B.

COMPRESS SUPERARMOUR

Highlight SuperArmour, hold Right and press R, A, B, R, A, L, L, R, B, A.

COMPRESS TANGOSUPPORT

Highlight TangoSupport, hold Right and press L, B, L, A, B, L, A, B, A, L.

COMPRESS UNDERSHIRT

Highlight UnderShirt, hold Right and press A, R, B, B, R, L, R, A, L, A.

ANTI ELEC * NUMBERMAN CODE

Once the Numberman Machine is in Higsby's shop, use it and enter **35607360**.

ANTI FIRE * NUMBERMAN CODE

Once the Numberman Machine is in Higsby's shop, use it and enter **73877466**.

ANTI NAVI V NUMBERMAN CODE

Once the Numberman Machine is in Higsby's shop, use it and enter **05068930**.

ANTI SWORD R NUMBERMAN CODE

Once the Numberman Machine is in Higsby's shop, use it and enter **10386794**.

ANTI WATER * NUMBERMAN CODE

Once the Numberman Machine is in Higsby's shop, use it and enter **25465278**.

ANTI WOOD * NUMBERMAN CODE

Once the Numberman Machine is in Higsby's shop, use it and enter **10133670**.

ATTACK MAX (YELLOW NCP) NUMBERMAN CODE

Once the Numberman Machine is in Higsby's shop, use it and enter **63231870**.

BEATSUPPORT NCP NUMBERMAN CODE

Once the Numberman Machine is in Higsby's shop, use it and enter **79877132**.

BODY PACK NUMBERMAN CODE
Once the Numberman Machine is in Higsby's shop, use it and enter **30112002**.

BUSTERPACK NCP NUMBERMAN CODE
Once the Numberman Machine is in Higsby's shop, use it and enter **80246758**.

CHARGE MAX (WHITE NCP) NUMBERMAN CODE
Once the Numberman Machine is in Higsby's shop, use it and enter **87412146**.

CUSTOM 2 NUMBERMAN CODE
Once the Numberman Machine is in Higsby's shop, use it and enter **15595587**.

CUSTOM BOLT 3 G NUMBERMAN CODE
Once the Numberman Machine is in Higsby's shop, use it and enter **07765623**.

DARK INVIS * NUMBERMAN CODE
Once the Numberman Machine is in Higsby's shop, use it and enter **68799876**.

DJANGOSP D NUMBERMAN CODE
Once the Numberman Machine is in Higsby's shop, use it and enter **91098051**.

FULL ENERGY NUMBERMAN CODE
Once the Numberman Machine is in Higsby's shop, use it and enter **12118790**.

FULL ENERGY NUMBERMAN CODE
Once the Numberman Machine is in Higsby's shop, use it and enter **90914896**.

GUN DEL SOL 3 O NUMBERMAN CODE
Once the Numberman Machine is in Higsby's shop, use it and enter **35321321**.

HP +200 (PINK NCP) NUMBERMAN CODE
Once the Numberman Machine is in Higsby's shop, use it and enter **90630807**.

HP+300 (WHITE NCP) NUMBERMAN CODE
Once the Numberman Machine is in Higsby's shop, use it and enter
13926561.

HP+400 (PINK NCP) NUMBERMAN CODE
Once the Numberman Machine is in Higsby's shop, use it and enter
03419893.

HP+400 NCP NUMBERMAN CODE
Once the Numberman Machine is in Higsby's shop, use it and enter
45654128.

HP+50 NCP NUMBERMAN CODE
Once the Numberman Machine is in Higsby's shop, use it and enter
31084443.

HP+500 (WHITE NCP) NUMBERMAN CODE
Once the Numberman Machine is in Higsby's shop, use it and enter
72846472.

LOCK ENEMY NUMBERMAN CODE
Once the Numberman Machine is in Higsby's shop, use it and enter
29789661.

RAPID MAX (PINK NCP) NUMBERMAN CODE
Once the Numberman Machine is in Higsby's shop, use it and enter
36695497.

RECOVERY-300 Y NUMBERMAN CODE
Once the Numberman Machine is in Higsby's shop, use it and enter
18746897.

RUSHSUPPORT NCP NUMBERMAN CODE
Once the Numberman Machine is in Higsby's shop, use it and enter
09609807.

SHINOBI DASH NUMBERMAN CODE
Once the Numberman Machine is in Higsby's shop, use it and enter
64892292.

SOULTIME +1 (YELLOW NCP) NUMBERMAN CODE
Once the Numberman Machine is in Higsby's shop, use it and enter
28256341.

SPIN BLUE NUMBERMAN CODE

Once the Numberman Machine is in Higsby's shop, use it and enter **12541883**.

SPIN GREEN NUMBERMAN CODE

Once the Numberman Machine is in Higsby's shop, use it and enter **78987728**.

SPIN RED NUMBERMAN CODE

Once the Numberman Machine is in Higsby's shop, use it and enter **30356451**.

STATIC S NUMBERMAN CODE

Once the Numberman Machine is in Higsby's shop, use it and enter **48958798**.

TANGOSUPPORT NCP NUMBERMAN CODE

Once the Numberman Machine is in Higsby's shop, use it and enter **54288793**.

UNLOCKER NUMBERMAN CODE

Once the Numberman Machine is in Higsby's shop, use it and enter **64664560**.

UNLOCKER NUMBERMAN CODE

Once the Numberman Machine is in Higsby's shop, use it and enter **28706568**.

UNLOCKER NUMBERMAN CODE

Once the Numberman Machine is in Higsby's shop, use it and enter **73978713**.

UNTRAP NUMBERMAN CODE

Once the Numberman Machine is in Higsby's shop, use it and enter **00798216**.

MONSTER FORCE

RESTART LEVEL
Pause the game, hold L + R and press A.

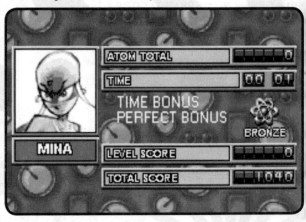

FINISH LEVEL
During a game, hold L + R + A and press Up.

PLAY AS MINA OR DREW
At the Character Select, hold L + R + B and press Right.

NICKTOONS UNITE!

LEVEL 2 : FENTON LAB
Select Continue and enter **JAZMINE**.

LEVEL 3 : VLAD'S CHATEAU
Select Continue and enter **PAULINA**.

LEVEL 4 : BIKINI BOTTOM
Select Continue and enter **SKULKER**.

LEVEL 5 : CHUM BUCKET
Select Continue and enter **PATRICK**.

LEVEL 6 : PLANKTON
Select Continue and enter **MERMAID**.

LEVEL 7 : TIMMY'S HOME
Select Continue and enter **SCALLOP**.

LEVEL 8 : DIMMSDALE DUMP
Select Continue and enter **BABYSIT**.

LEVEL 9 : CROCKER'S LOCKER ROOM
Select Continue and enter **GODDARD**.

LEVEL 10 : JIMMY'S LAB
Select Continue and enter **ESTEVEZ**.

LEVEL 11 : SUBTERRANEAN CAVES
Select Continue and enter **LIBERTY**.

LEVEL 12 : PROF CALAMITOUS' LAB
Select Continue and enter **SKYLARK**.

POWER RANGERS: SPACE PATROL DELTA

EPISODE 1 ON EASY
Enter **ZZB** as a password.

EPISODE 2A ON EASY
Enter **ZVC** as a password.

EPISODE 2B ON EASY
Enter **QZB** as a password.

EPISODE 3A ON EASY
Enter **QVC** as a password.

0G EPISODE 3B ON EASY
Enter **!** as a password.

XH EPISODE 4A ON EASY
Enter **!** as a password.

EPISODE 4B ON EASY
Enter **R0G** as a password.

EPISODE 5A ON EASY
Enter **Z2B** as a password.

EPISODE 5B ON EASY
Enter **V6C** as a password.

EPISODE 6A ON EASY
Enter **L6C** as a password.

4G EPISODE 6B ON EASY
Enter **!** as a password.

EPISODE 7A ON EASY
Enter **R4G** as a password.

EPISODE 7B ON EASY
Enter **M8H** as a password.

EPISODE 8A ON EASY
Enter **0BF** as a password.

EPISODE 8B ON EASY
Enter SGD as a password.

FINAL BATTLE ON EASY
Enter **SBF** as a password.

RIVER CITY RANSOM EX

Select the status menu and change your name to the following:

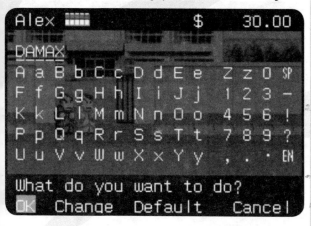

MAX STATS
DAMAX

$999999.99
PLAYA

CUSTOM CHAR
XTRA0

CUSTOM SELF
XTRA1

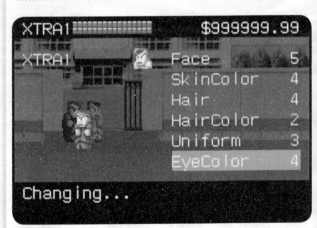

CUSTOM MOVE
  XTRA2

CLEAR SAVE
  ERAZE

TECHNIQUES 1

FUZZY. This group includes Mach Punch, Dragon Kick, Acro Circus, Grand Slam, Javelin Man, Slick Trick, Nitro Port, Twin Kick, Deadly Shot, Top Spin, Helicopter, Torpedo.

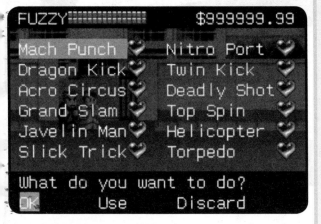

TECHNIQUES 2

WUZZY. This group includes Slap Happy, Pulper, Headbutt, Kickstand, Big Bang, Wheel Throw, Glide Chop, Head Bomb, Chain Chump, Jet Kick, Shuriken, Flip Throw.

TECHNIQUES 3

WAZZA. This group includes Boomerang, Charge It, Bat Fang, Flying Kick, Speed Drop, Bomb Blow, Killer Kick, Bike Kick, Slam Punk, Dragon Knee, God Fist, Hyperguard.

TECHNIQUES 4

BEAR*. This group includes PhoenixWing, Inlines, Springlines, Rocketeers, Air Merc's Narcishoes, Magic Pants, Pandora Box, Skaterz, Custom Fit.

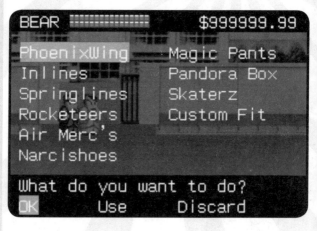

ROAD RASH: JAILBREAK

ALL CHARACTERS AT LEVEL 4 AND ALL RACES
Press Select at the Player select and enter **ALAKAZAMM**.

ALL RACES
Press Select at the Player select and enter **KEEPOUT**.

ALL RACES IN COP PATROL
Press Select at the Player select and enter **FELONY**.

SURVIVAL
Press Select at the Player select and enter **MENACE**.

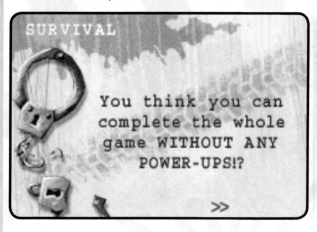

ACE LEVEL 2
Press Select at the Player select and enter **SWING**.

ACE LEVEL 3
Press Select at the Player select and enter **FLUSH**.

ACE LEVEL 4
Press Select at the Player select and enter **BRUISE**.

FAT HOAGIE
Press Select at the Player select and enter **EDGY**.

FAT HOAGIE LEVEL 2
Press Select at the Player select and enter **SLAP**.

FAT HOAGIE LEVEL 3
Press Select at the Player select and enter **FURIOUS**.

FAT HOAGIE LEVEL 4

Press Select at the Player select and enter **HEADACHE**.

HURL LEVEL 1

Press Select at the Player select and enter **HOWDY**.

HURL LEVEL 2

Press Select at the Player select and enter **PULSE**.

HURL LEVEL 3

Press Select at the Player select and enter **STRIDER**.

HURL LEVEL 4

Press Select at the Player select and enter **BEATNIK**.

LULU LEVEL 2
Press Select at the Player select and enter **BLOW**.

LULU LEVEL 3
Press Select at the Player select and enter **SCOURGE**.

LULU LEVEL 4
Press Select at the Player select and enter **QUICKEN**.

TINY LEVEL 2
Press Select at the Player select and enter **AXLE**.

TINY LEVEL 3
Press Select at the Player select and enter **WHEEL**.

TINY LEVEL 4
Press Select at the Player select and enter **PROPER**.

ROAD TRIP: SHIFTING GEARS

DRAGON PARTS
Complete the Angel Cup. Select Change Name from the Options and enter **DRAGON**.

RUGRATS: I GOTTA GO PARTY

GO TO LEVEL 2
Enter **CBKBBB** as a password.

GO TO LEVEL 3
Enter **RBHBNB** as a password.

GO TO LEVEL 4
Enter **SNFBBC** as a password.

GO TO LEVEL 5
Enter **TNHHBG** as a password.

GO TO LEVEL 6
Enter **VNFTNG** as a password.

GO TO LEVEL 7
Enter **XNHTFC** as a password.

GO TO LEVEL 8
Enter **ZNFTRJ** as a password.

SECRET AGENT BARBIE: ROYAL JEWELS MISSION

ALL SECRETS
Enter **TTTTTS** as a password.

ENGLAND – THE ROYAL TOWER
Enter **BBBBCG** as a password.

ENGLAND – STREET CHASE
Enter **DBBFCM** as a password.

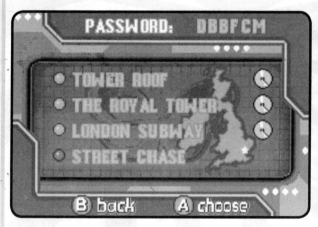

CHINA – CITY STREETS
Enter **FBBFFQ** as a password.

CHINA – SECRET HIDEOUT
Enter **GBBPFH** as a password.

CHINA – GOLDEN CITY
Enter **HBBPKN** as a password.

CHINA – THE PALACE
Enter **JCBPKQ** as a password.

ITALY – OPERA HOUSE
Enter **KCBTKC** as a password.

ITALY - CANAL CHASE
Enter **LCGTKJ** as a password.

ITALY – FASHION DISTRICT
Enter **MCHTKL** as a password.

ITALY – SCUBA SEARCH
Enter **NCHTTC** as a password.

MEXICO - SUNNY CITY
Enter **PCRTTN** as a password.

SEGA SMASH PACK

ECCO THE DOLPHIN
Pause the game with Ecco facing the screen and press Right, B, R, B, R, Down, R, Up. This unlocks Stage Select, Sound Select, and Unlimited Lives.

GOLDEN AXE
Select arcade mode and hold Down/Left + B and press **START** at the Character Select screen. This unlocks Level Select.

GOLDEN AXE
Select arcade mode and hold Down/Left + A + R. Release the buttons and press **START** to gain Nine Continues.

SONIC SPINBALL
At the Options screen, press A, Down, B, Down, R, Down, A, B, Up, A, R, Up, B, R, Up. This unlocks Level Select. The following commands will start you at that level.

LEVEL	COMMAND
2 Lava Powerhouse	Hold A and press **START**
3 The Machine	Hold B and press **START**
4 Showdown	Hold R and press **START**

SONIC SPINBALL
At the Options screen, press A, Up, R, Up, L, Up, A, R, Down, A, L, Down, R, L, Down. This unlocks the game's Credits.

SHAMAN KING: LEGACY OF THE SPIRITS, SOARING HAWK

SPIRIT OF FIRE

At the title screen, press Right, Right, L, Left + R, Down, R, Right, B.

SHAMAN KING: LEGACY OF THE SPIRITS, SPRINTING WOLF

SPIRIT OF FIRE

At the title screen, press Right, Right, L, Left + R, Down, R, Right, B.

SHINING SOUL

2 EXTRA HERBS

Enter your name as **Shining**.

2 VALUING SCROLLS

Enter your name as **Force**.

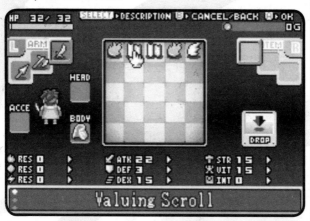

HEALING DROP

Enter your name as **Soul**.

MONKEY DOLL

Enter your name as **AiAi**.

PAINTER'S SOUL

Enter your name as **Salamander**.

JUDO UNIFORM FOR DRAGONUTE

Select the Dragonute and enter your name as **Segata**.

LEAF BRIEFS FOR ARCHER

Select the Archer and enter your name as **NomuNomu**.

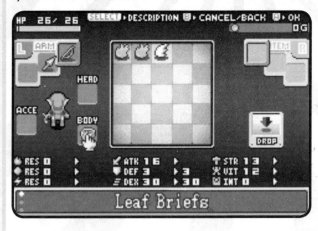

SHINING SOUL II

DREAM HAT

Enter **Nindri** as your name.

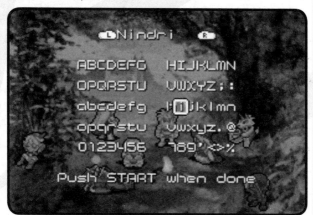

Dream Hat

GENOME RING

Enter **Genomes** as your name.

Genome Ring

ATLUS RING

Enter **Vjum** as your name.

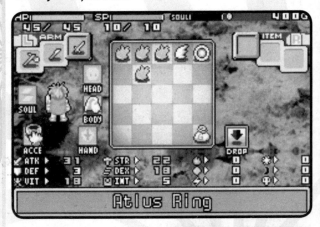

POWER GLOVES

Enter **VJxSS** as your name.

STR +5

Enter **Ninky** as your name.

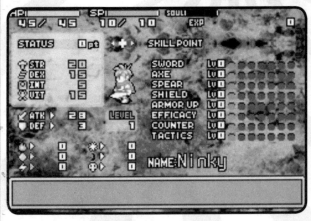

DEX +5

Enter **Yoshi** as your name.

VIT +5

Enter **Taicho** as your name.

INT +5, RTH +30

Enter **Dengeki** as your name.

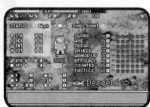

RDK +30

Enter **Montaka** as your name.

RFR +30

Enter **Iyoku** as your name.

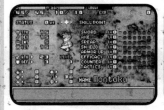 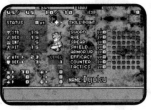

RIC +30

Enter **Mizupin** as your name.

RPO +30

Enter **Hachi** as your name.

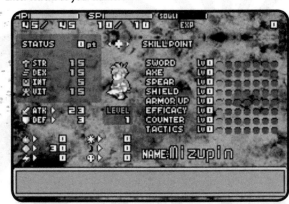

SPIDER-MAN 2

INVINCIBILITY
At the title screen, press Up, Down, Right, A.

LEVEL SELECT
After completing the game, start a new game with the name
FLUWDEAR.

SPYRO ORANGE: THE CORTEX CONSPIRACY

100 GEMS
At the Mode menu, press L + R, then enter **V1S10NS**.

ORANGE GAME
At the Mode menu, press L + R, then enter **SP4RX**.

PURPLE GAME
At the Mode menu, press L + R, then enter **P0RT4L**.

ORANGE SPYRO
At the Mode menu, press L + R, then enter **SPYRO**.

SHEEP MODE
At the Mode menu, press L + R, then enter **SH33P**.

SHEEP FLAME MODE
At the Mode menu, press L + R, then enter **B41S0KV**.

CRASH PARTY USA MINI-GAME

Start up your Game Boy Advance and hold L + R.

STREET FIGHTER ALPHA 3

ALL FIGHTERS

At the title screen, press Left, Right, Down, Right, L, L, A, L, L, B, R, A, Up.

ALL MODES

At the title screen, press A, Up, A, L, R, Right, L, Right, A, Down, Right.

Now press L, Right, A, R, Up, L, Right, B, A, Up, Right, Down, Right.

PLAY AS SUPER BISON

At the character select, hold **START** and select Bison.

PLAY AS SHIN AKUMA

At the character select, hold **START** and select Akuma.

ALTERNATE COSTUMES

At the character select, press L or R.

FINAL BATTLE

At the speed select, hold A + B.

SUPER MONKEY BALL JR.

ENABLE ALL

At the Title screen, press Down, Down, Up, Up, Left, Right, Left, Right, B, A.

BLOCKY MODE

At the Title screen, press Left, Left, Right, Right, Down, Down, A.

NICE TRY

At the Title screen, press Up, Up, Down, Down, Left, Right, Left, Right, B, A.

SUPER PUZZLE FIGHTER 2 TURBO

AKUMA PLAYER 1
Highlight Morrigan, hold SELECT, press Down (3x), Left (3x), A.

AKUMA PLAYER 2
Highlight Felicia, hold SELECT, press Down (3x), Right (3x), A.

ANITA PLAYER 1
Highlight Morrigan, hold SELECT, move to Donovan and press A.

ANITA PLAYER 2
Highlight Felicia, hold SELECT, move to Donovan and press A.

DAN PLAYER 1
Highlight Morrigan, hold SELECT, press Left (3x), Down (3x), A.

DAN PLAYER 2
Highlight Felicia, hold SELECT, press Right (3x), Down (3x), A

DEVILOT

Highlight Morrigan, hold SELECT, press Left (3x), Down (3x), A as the timer hits 10.

HSIEN-KO'S PAPER TALISMAN PLAYER 1

Highlight Morrigan, hold SELECT, move to Hsien-Ko and press A.

HSIEN-KO'S PAPER TALISMAN PLAYER 2

Highlight Felicia, hold SELECT, move to Hsien-Ko and press A.

THAT'S SO RAVEN 2: SUPERNATURAL STYLE

COSTUME MODE
At the title screen, press Left, Right, Up, Down, B, B, B, Up, Down.

UNLIMITED ENERGY MODE
At the title screen, press B, B, L, R, Up, Down, Up, Left, Right.

TOM AND JERRY: THE MAGIC RING

LEVEL 1-1 AS JERRY
Enter **1236** as a password.

LEVEL 1-2 AS JERRY
Enter **6878** as a password.

LEVEL 1-3 AS JERRY
Enter **5121** as a password.

LEVEL 1-4 AS JERRY
Enter **2753** as a password.

LEVEL 1-5 AS JERRY
Enter **7616** as a password.

LEVEL 2 AS JERRY
Enter **7531** as a password.

LEVEL 3 AS JERRY
Enter **8358** as a password.

LEVEL 4-1 AS JERRY
Enter **1176** as a password.

LEVEL 4-2 AS JERRY
Enter **6718** as a password.

LEVEL 4-3 AS JERRY
Enter **5261** as a password.

LEVEL 5 AS JERRY
Enter **8251** as a password.

LEVEL 6 AS JERRY
Enter **2761** as a password.

LEVEL 7-1 AS JERRY
Enter **2856** as a password.

LEVEL 7-2 AS JERRY
Enter **5228** as a password.

LEVEL 1-1 AS TOM
Enter **5488** as a password.

LEVEL 1-2 AS TOM
Enter **4121** as a password.

LEVEL 1-3 AS TOM
Enter **1353** as a password.

LEVEL 1-4 AS TOM
Enter **8246** as a password.

LEVEL 1-5 AS TOM
Enter **3868** as a password.

LEVEL 2 AS TOM
Enter **3783** as a password.

LEVEL 3 AS TOM
Enter **5423** as a password.

LEVEL 4-1 AS TOM
Enter **5348** as a password.

LEVEL 4-2 AS TOM
Enter **4281** as a password.

LEVEL 4-3 AS TOM
Enter **1413** as a password.

LEVEL 5 AS TOM
Enter **5126** as a password.

LEVEL 6 AS TOM
Enter **8238** as a password.

LEVEL 7-1 AS TOM
Enter **8143** as a password.

LEVEL 7-2 AS TOM
Enter **1456** as a password.

TOMB RAIDER: THE PROPHECY

CREDITS

Enter **ARIA** as a password.

PASSWORDS

LEVEL	PASSWORD
1	PRLD
2	GAZE
3	MEDI
4	HAXE
5	PATH
6	BONE
7	TREE
8	LINK
9	KURZ
10	HELL
11	WEFX
12	MEMO
13	HEAR
14	FITZ
15	ELRC
16	CLIK
17	MGSL
18	ROMA
19	MONK
20	AEON
21	TIME
22	OLIM
23	LAND
24	DART
25	HILL
26	CHEX
27	STLK
28	MECH
29	ARKD
30	MUSH
31	LITH

TONY HAWK'S UNDERGROUND

SKIP TUTORIAL

At the Main Menu, hold R and press Left, Down, **START**, **START**, Right, Up, Up, L, Down.

TONY HAWK'S UNDERGROUND 2

TENNIS SHOOTER MINIGAME

Once you unlock Bam's character on the map, talk to him. Knock down the rollerbladers, then go back. He'll give you the Tennis Shooter minigame. Once you've completed three levels, save your game to access Tennis Shooter at any time from the main menu.

TOP GUN: COMBAT ZONES

LEVEL 2 - PACIFIC OCEAN ON EASY

Enter **9799** as a password.

LEVEL 3 - NORTHERN SIBERIA ON EASY

Enter **8457** as a password.

LEVEL 4 - BERING STRAIT ON EASY

Enter **6767** as a password.

LEVEL 5 - NORTH SEA ON EASY

Enter **6891** as a password.

LEVEL 6 - EASTERN EUROPE ON EASY

Enter **2468** as a password.

LEVEL 7 - ARABIAN PENINSULA ON EASY

Enter **4479** as a password.

LEVEL 8 - SOUTHEAST ASIA ON EASY

Enter **3232** as a password.

LEVEL 9 - MONGOLIAN DESERT ON EASY

Enter **1295** as a password.

LEVEL 10 - ARCTIC CIRCLE ON EASY

Enter **7783** as a password.

LEVEL 11 - SOUTH AMERICA ON EASY
Enter **8226** as a password.

LEVEL 12 - GULF OF MEXICO ON EASY
Enter **7453** as a password.

LEVEL 2 - PACIFIC OCEAN ON NORMAL
Enter **7294** as a password.

LEVEL 3 - NORTHERN SIBERIA ON NORMAL
Enter **4947** as a password.

LEVEL 4 - BERING STRAIT ON NORMAL
Enter **1599** as a password.

LEVEL 5 - NORTH SEA ON NORMAL
Enter **9145** as a password.

LEVEL 6 - EASTERN EUROPE ON NORMAL
Enter **8813** as a password.

LEVEL 7 - ARABIAN PENINSULA ON NORMAL
Enter **9915** as a password.

LEVEL 8 - SOUTHEAST ASIA ON NORMAL
Enter **8212** as a password.

LEVEL 9 - MONGOLIAN DESERT ON NORMAL
Enter **9215** as a password.

LEVEL 10 - ARCTIC CIRCLE ON NORMAL
Enter **4518** as a password.

LEVEL 11 - SOUTH AMERICA ON NORMAL
Enter **2121** as a password.

LEVEL 12 - GULF OF MEXICO ON NORMAL
Enter **4211** as a password.

LEVEL 2 - PACIFIC OCEAN ON HARD
Enter **3468** as a password.

LEVEL 3 - NORTHERN SIBERIA ON HARD
Enter **2345** as a password.

LEVEL 4 - BERING STRAIT ON HARD
Enter **8791** as a password.

LEVEL 5 - NORTH SEA ON HARD
Enter **6642** as a password.

LEVEL 6 - EASTERN EUROPE ON HARD
Enter **2918** as a password.

LEVEL 7 - ARABIAN PENINSULA ON HARD
Enter **5748** as a password.

LEVEL 8 - SOUTHEAST ASIA ON HARD
Enter **5367** as a password.

LEVEL 9 - MONGOLIAN DESERT ON HARD
Enter **3783** as a password.

LEVEL 10 - ARCTIC CIRCLE ON HARD
Enter **9818** as a password.

LEVEL 11 - SOUTH AMERICA ON HARD
Enter **9319** as a password.

LEVEL 12 - GULF OF MEXICO ON HARD
Enter **6161** as a password.

TRON 2.0: KILLER APP

ALL MINIGAMES
At the title screen, press Left, Left, Left, Left, Up, Right, Down, Down, Select.

URBAN YETI

UNLOCK EVERYTHING
Enter **TONYGOLD** as a password.

DISCUS TOURNAMENT
Enter **PINGPONG** as a password.

LAZY SEWER O' FUN
Enter **YETIRAFT** as a password.

SOUP KITCHEN MANAGER
Enter **HAMSTEAK** as a password.

YETI CHICKEN RANCHER
Enter **PROVIDER** as a password.

START AT LEVEL 1
  Enter **BUZZWORD** as a password.

START AT LEVEL 2
  Enter **FOREWORD** as a password.

START AT LEVEL 3
  Enter **COOKBOOK** as a password.

START AT LEVEL 4
  Enter **FEEDBAGS** as a password.

START AT LEVEL 5
  Enter **HAMSTEAK** as a password.

START AT LEVEL 6
  Enter **DAYBREAK** as a password.

START AT LEVEL 7
  Enter **SUNLIGHT** as a password.

START AT LEVEL 8
  Enter **NITETIME** as a password.

START AT LEVEL 9
  Enter **EASTSIDE** as a password.

START AT LEVEL 10
  Enter **BEATDOWN** as a password.

START AT LEVEL 11
  Enter **VENGEFUL** as a password.

START AT LEVEL 12
  Enter **FRISBEES** as a password.

START AT LEVEL 13
  Enter **ICESKATE** as a password.

START AT LEVEL 14
  Enter **PINGPONG** as a password.

START AT LEVEL 15
  Enter **DOWNTOWN** as a password.

START AT LEVEL 16
  Enter **CITYMAPS** as a password.

START AT LEVEL 17
 Enter **DUMPSTER** as a password.

START AT LEVEL 18
 Enter **WATERWAY** as a password.

START AT LEVEL 19
 Enter **TIRETUBE** as a password.

START AT LEVEL 20
 Enter **YETIRAFT** as a password.

START AT LEVEL 21
 Enter **SUBURBIA** as a password.

START AT LEVEL 22
 Enter **HOUSETOP** as a password.

START AT LEVEL 23
 Enter **CITIZENS** as a password.

START AT LEVEL 24
 Enter **CHICKENS** as a password.

START AT LEVEL 25
 Enter **SONGBIRD** as a password.

START AT LEVEL 26
 Enter **PROVIDER** as a password.

STRANGE COLORS AND SOUND
 Enter **BSWSBSWS** as a password.

THE URBZ: SIMS IN THE CITY

CLUB XIZZLE
Once you gain access to Club Xizzle, enter with the password
"bucket."

WINNIE THE POOH'S RUMBLY TUMBLY ADVENTURE

GAME COMPLETED
Enter **3013736** as a password.

EEYORE'S FIRST AREA
Enter **9744991** as a password.

EEYORE'S SECOND AREA
Enter **9301241** as a password.

EEYORE'S THIRD AREA
Enter **3220311** as a password.

EEYORE'S AREA COMPLETE
Enter **3412121** as a password.

PIGLET'S FIRST AREA
Enter **5735172** as a password.

PIGLET'S SECOND AREA
Enter **7045732** as a password.

PIGLET'S THIRD AREA
Enter **1156612** as a password.

PIGLET'S AREA COMPLETE
Enter **1348422** as a password.

POOH'S FIRST AREA
Enter **1937986** as a password.

POOH'S SECOND AREA
Enter **1388596** as a password.

POOH'S THIRD AREA
Enter **5399476** as a password.

ROO'S FIRST AREA
Enter **3412773** as a password.

ROO'S SECOND AREA
Enter **9999053** as a password.

ROO'S THIRD AREA
Enter **5505553** as a password.

ROO'S AREA COMPLETE
Enter **3011033** as a password.

TIGGER'S FIRST AREA
Enter **7847570** as a password.

TIGGER'S SECOND AREA
Enter **5560830** as a password.

TIGGER'S THIRD AREA
Enter **3834540** as a password.

TIGGER'S FOURTH AREA
Enter **9172120** as a password.

TIGGER'S AREA COMPLETE
Enter **1749510** as a password.

WORLD CHAMPIONSHIP POKER

10 MILLION DOLLAR
Enter the following as a password: 7 Hearts, King Spades, 2 Hearts, Queen Clubs, 9 Hearts, Jack Hearts.

XXX

INFINITE HEALTH AND AMMUNITION
After completing Level 12, select Extras to find Infinite Health and Ammunition.

YOSHI TOPSY-TURVY

CHALLENGE MODE AND CHALLENGE 1
Defeat Bowser for the 2nd time in story mode.

CHALLENGES 2, 3, 4
Complete the Egg Gallery in story mode.

FINAL CHALLENGE
Earn all Golds in story mode.

YU-GI-OH! DESTINY BOARD TRAVELER

GRANDPA
At the Title screen, press L, Right + B, Right, B, R, Left, Down, A.

KAIBAMAN
At the Title screen, press Down, B, Left, Right, Right, R, Up + R, A.

YAMI BAKURA
At the Title screen, press L, Down, Right, Left + B, R, Down, Down, A.

YAMI YUGI
At the Title screen, press R, Left, B, Right, Up + R, Right, Down, A.

YU-GI-OH! 7 TRIALS TO GLORY: WORLD CHAMPIONSHIP TOURNAMENT 2005

PURPLE TITLE SCREEN
Completing the game changes the title screen from blue to purple. To switch it back, press Up, Up, Down, Down, Left, Right, Left, Right, B, A at the title screen.

CREDITS
Defeat the game. Then, press Up, Up, Down, Down, Left, Right, Left, Right, B, A.

CARD PASSWORDS
At the password machine, press R and enter the following.

CARD	PASSWORD
30,000-Year White Turtle	11714098
7 Colored Fish	23771716
7 Completed	86198326
A Hero Emerges	21597117
Acid Trap Hole	41356845
Air Eater	08353769
Alligator's Sword	64428736
Alligator's Sword Dragon	03366982
Alpha The Magnet Warrior	99785935
Amazon Archer	91869203
Amazon of the Seas	17968114
Amphibian Beast	67371383
Amphibious Bugroth	40173854

CARD	PASSWORD
Ancient Brain	42431843
Ancient Elf	93221206
Ancient Lizard Warrior	43230671
Anti Raigeki	42364257
Aqua Chorus	95132338
Aqua Dragon	86164529
Archfiend Soldier	49881766
Arma Knight	36151751
Armaill	53153481
Armed Ninja	09076207
Armored Lizard	15480588
Armored Rat	16246527
Armored Starfish	17535588
Armored Zombie	20277860
Axe of Despair	40619825
Axe Raider	48305365
Baby Dragon	88819587
Banisher of the Light	61528025
Baron of the Fiend Sword	86325596
Barrel Dragon	81480460
Barrel Lily	67841515
Barrel Rock	10476868
Beaver Warrior	32452818
Beta The Magnet Warrior	39256679
Bite Shoes	50122883
Black Luster Soldier - Envoy of the Beginning	72989439
Black Pendant	65169794
Bladefly	28470714
Blast Sphere	26302522
Blue Eyes Toon Dragon	53183600
Blue Eyes White Dragon	89631139
Boneheimer	98456117
Book of SecretArts	91595718
Bottom Dweller	81386177
Catapult Turtle	95727991
Celtic Guardian	91152256
Ceremonial Bell	20228463
Change of Heart	04031928

CARD	PASSWORD
Chaos Emperor Dragon - EotE	82301904
Crass Clown	93889755
Curse of the Masked Beast	94377247
Cyber Falcon	30655537
Cyber Harpie	80316585
Cyber Jar	34124316
Cyber Shield	63224564
Cyber Soldier of Darkworld	75559356
Cyber-Stein	69015963
Cyber-Tech Alligator	48766543
D.D. Warrior Lady	07572887
Dark Artist	72520073
Dark Illusion Ritual	41426869
Dark-Eyes Illusionist	38247752
Darkfire Soldier #1	05388481
Darkfire Soldier #2	78861134
Des Koala	69579761
Destroyer Golem	73481154
Dissolverock	40826495
Dragonic Attack	32437102
Durnames Dark Witch	12493482
Eatgaboon	42578427
Exile of the Wicked	26725158
Exodia the Forbidden One	33396948
Fiend Reflection #2	02863439
Final Destiny	18591904
Firegrass	53293545
Flame Champion	42599677
Flash Assailant	96890582
Flower Wolf	95952802
Flying Kamakiri #1	84834865
Flying Kamakiri #2	03134241
Gaia the Fierce Knight	06368038
Gamma The Magnet Warrior	11549357
Garnecia Elefantis	49888191
Gemini Elf	69140098
Giant Flea	41762634
Giant Rat	97017120
Gift of the Mystical Elf	98299011

CARD	PASSWORD
Graverobber's Retribution	33737664
Great White	13429800
Harpie Lady	76812113
Headless Knight	05434080
Humanoid Worm Drake	05600127
Hyosube	02118022
Hyozanryu	62397231
Illusion Wall	13945283
Iron Blacksmith Kotetsu	73431236
Jellyfish	14851496
Jinzo	77585513
Jowgen the Spiritualist	41855169
Karate Man	23289281
Kojikocy	01184620
Kuriboh	40640057
La Jinn	97590747
Lady of Faith	17358176
Lady Panther	38480590
Last Day of Witch	90330453
Lava Battleguard	20394040
Left Arm of the Forbidden One	07902349
Left Leg of the Forbidden One	44519536
Little Chimera	68658728
Luminous Spark	81777047
Mad Dog of Darkness	79182538
Mad Sword Beast	79870141
Magic Swordsman Neo	50930991
Magical Scientist	34206604
Magician of Faith	31560081
Malevolent Nuzzler	99597615
Man Eating Treasure Chest	13723605
Manga Ryu Ran	38369349
Marauding Captain	02460565
Mask of Darkness	28933734
Mechanicalchaser	07359741
Melchid the Four-Face Beast	86569121
Metal Guardian	68339286
Millennium Shield	32012841
Milus Radiant	07489323

CARD	PASSWORD
Monster Reborn	83764718
Mother Grizzly	57839750
Mystic Plasma Zone	18161786
Mystic Tomato	83011277
Offerings to the Doomed	19230407
Ooguchi	58861941
Overdrive	02311603
Pendulum Machine	24433920
Pinch Hopper	26185991
Pot of Greed	55144522
Red-Eyes Black Dragon	74677422
Red-Eyes Black Metal Dragon	64335804
Reflect Bounder	02851070
Relinquished	64631466
Restructer Revolution	99518961
Right Arm of the Forbidden One	70903634
Right Leg of the Forbidden One	08124921
Robbin' Zombie	83258273
Rogue Doll	91939608
Ryu Ran	02964201
Ryu-Kishin Powered	24611934
Shining Abyss	87303357
Shining Angel	95956346
Shining Friendship	82085619
Silver Fang	90357090
Sinister Serpent	08131171
Skull Mark Ladybug	64306248
Skull Servant	32274490
Slate Warrior	78636495
Slot Machine	03797883
Soul of Purity and Light	77527210
Soul Release	05758500
Spear Dragon	31553716
Spike Bot	87511987
Spirit of Flames	13522325
St. Joan	21175632
Sword of Deep-Seated	98495314
Swords of Revealing Light	72302403
Tainted Wisdom	28725004

CARD	PASSWORD
Talwar Demon	11761845
The 13th Grave	00032864
The All-Seeing White Tiger	32269855
The Bistro Butcher	71107816
The Earl of Demise	66989694
The Gross Ghost of Fled Dreams	68049471
The Portrait's Secret	32541773
The Shallow Grave	43434803
The Unhappy Maiden	51275027
Thousand Eyes Idol	27125110
Thousand Eyes Relinquised	63519819
Time Seal	85316708
Tornado Bird	71283180
Total Defense Shogun	75372290
Tribe Infecting Virus	33184167
Turtle Tiger	37313348
Two-Headed King Rex	94119974
UFO Turtle	60806437
Ultimate Offering	80604091
Ushi Oni	48649353
Vorse Raider	14898066
Water Omotics	02483611
Wingweaver	31447217
Yata-Garusa	03078576

ZOIDS: LEGACY

CYCLOPES TYPE ONE/TWO, DIABLO TIGER DATA AND ZOID CORES TO BUILD THEM

Complete the game. Then, at the title screen, press L, L, R, R, Up, Down, Up, Down, Left, Left, R, R, Right, Right, Left, Up, **START**.

GILVADER, KING GOJULA ZI DATA AND ZOID CORES TO BUILD THEM

Complete the game. Then, at the title screen, press R, R, L, L, Down, Up, Down, Up, Right, Right, L, L, Left, Left, Right, Down, **START**.

Everyone

ADVANCE WARS: DUAL STRIKE

ASPHALT URBAN GT

KIRBY: CANVAS CURSE

METROID PRIME PINBALL

NINTENDOGS

PAC-PIX

PING PALS

PUYO POP FEVER

RIDGE RACER DS

SPIDER-MAN 2

TIGER WOODS PGA TOUR

THE URBZ: SIMS IN THE CITY

YU-GI-OH! NIGHTMARE TROUBADOUR

ZOO KEEPER

E 10+

STAR WARS EPISODE III: REVENGE OF THE SITH

Teen

CASTLEVANIA: DAWN OF SORROW

FEEL THE MAGIC: XY/XX

TOM CLANCY'S SPLINTER CELL CHAOS THEORY

TRAUMA CENTER: UNDER THE KNIFE

NINTENDO DS™

Nintendo DS™ Table of Contents

ADVANCE WARS: DUAL STRIKE

ADVANCE WARS MAP

Select Map from the Design Room menu and immediately press and hold L + R. You will get a map that spells out Advance Wars.

By having old versions of advance wars inserted in your DS at the same time as Duel Strike, unlock new buyables at the the Battle Maps Shop!Unlockable How to Unlock

Select Battle Maps

ADVANCE WARPAPER

Insert Advance Wars in the GBA slot of your Nintendo DS. Start Advance Wars: Dual Strike. Select Battle maps and purchase Advance Warpaper. Select Display from the Design Room and choose Classic 1.

HACHI'S LAND

Insert Advance Wars in the GBA slot of your Nintendo DS. Start Advance Wars: Dual Strike. Select Battle Maps and purchase Hachi's Land for 1.

NELL'S LAND

Insert Advance Wars in the GBA slot of your Nintendo DS. Start Advance Wars: Dual Strike. Select Battle Maps and purchase Nell's Land for 1.

ADVANCE WARPAPER 2

Insert Advance Wars 2: Black Hole Rising in the GBA slot of your Nintendo DS. Start Advance Wars: Dual Strike. Select Battle maps and purchase Advance Warpaper 2. Select Display from the Design Room and choose Classic 2.

LASH'S LAND

Insert Advance Wars 2: Black Hole Rising in the GBA slot of your
Nintendo DS. Start Advance Wars: Dual Strike. Select Battle Maps
and purchase Lash's Land for 1.

STRUM'S LAND

Insert Advance Wars 2: Black Hole Rising in the GBA slot of your
Nintendo DS. Start Advance Wars: Dual Strike. Select Battle Maps
and purchase Strum's Land for 1.

ASPHALT URBAN GT

MONEY FOR NOTHING

Buy the Chevrolet 2005 Corvette C6 for $45,000. Then, go to your
garage and sell it for $45,500.

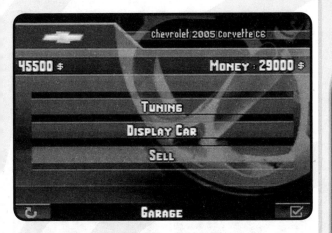

CASTLEVANIA: DAWN OF SORROW

POTION

Complete Boss Rush Mode.

RPG

Complete Boss Rush Mode in less than 5 minutes.

DEATH'S ROBE

Complete Boss Rush Mode in less than 6 minutes.

TERROR BEAR

Complete Boss Rush Mode in less than 7 minutes.

NUNCHAKUS

Complete Boss Rush Mode in less than 8 minutes.

FEEL THE MAGIC: XY/XX

RECORD YOUR VOICE ON THE TITLE SCREEN

While at the title screen, hold Down + Y to record whatever you want into the microphone. It will now play back whatever you recorded at random intervals while the title music plays. However, if you wish to play it back immediately, press Down + X. Down-Left + X will play it back slowly, while Down-Right + X will speed it up.

HARD MODE
Defeat the game on Normal difficulty.

HELL MODE
Defeat the game on Hard difficulty.

KIRBY: CANVAS CURSE

JUMP GAME
Defeat the game with all five characters. Select the game file to get Jump Game next to options on the main menu.

METROID PRIME PINBALL

PHAZON MINES
Complete Omega Pirate in Multi Mission Mode.

PHENDRANA DRIFTS
Complete Thardus in Multi Mission Mode.

NINTENDOGS

FEED DOG LIGHT BULB

When the light bulb appears above your dog, grab it and drag it to his/her mouth.

PAC-PIX

BUTTERFLY HIDDEN GESTURE

Select Sketchbook from the Gallery. Draw a figure eight. The drawing should fly upwards.

Practice gesture input. Try to find the hidden gestures available only in this mode!

CHERRIES HIDDEN GESTURE

Select Sketchbook from the Gallery. Draw a pair of cherries starting with one of the circles.

POGO STICK HIDDEN GESTURE

Select Sketchbook from the Gallery. Draw a P and it will bounce off the screen.

RAIN CLOUD HIDDEN GESTURE

Select Sketchbook from the Gallery. Draw a cloud and it will turn blue and rain will fall from the drawing.

SNAKE HIDDEN GESTURE

Select Sketchbook from the Gallery. Draw an a squiggly line. It will turn green and slither away.

TREBLE CLEF HIDDEN GESTURE

Select Sketchbook from the Gallery. Draw a treble clef.

SHOOT ARROWS AT PAC-MAN

After you have earned the Arrow gesture in Chapter 4, select Sketchbook from the Gallery. Draw an arrow facing Pac-man.

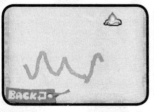

Practice gesture input. Try to find the hidden gestures available only in this mode!

PING PALS

50 COINS

Select Credits and let them run to the end.

HOLIDAY ITEMS

Set the date on your Nintendo DS to the following dates to get access to special Holiday Items:

DATE	ITEM	COST
February 14	Valentine (Boy)	300 Coins
February 14	Valentine (Girl)	200 Coins
February 21	Vessel Top	700 Coins
March 17	Snowflake	250 Coins
October 31	Bat Treats	400 Coins
October 31	Jack Hat	4000 Coins
October 31	Succubus	321 Coins
December 25	Elf Skirt	300 Coins
December 25	Jolly Suit	300 Coins
December 25	Merry Cap	10 Coins
Birthday	Birthday (Boy)	5 Coins
Birthday	Birthday (Girl)	5 Coins

SHANTAE BACKGROUND

Touch the Ping Pals logo exactly at midnight.

PUYO POP FEVER

ALL CHARACTERS AND CUTSCENES

Select Gallery from the Options. Highlight cutscene viewer, hold X and press Up, Down, Left, Right.

RIDGE RACER DS

00-AGENT CAR
Finish more than ten races in multi-player.

CADDY CAR
Finish more than ten races in multi-player.

GALAGA '88 CAR
Finish more than ten races in multi-player.

MARIO RACING CAR
Finish more than ten races in multi-player.

POOKA CAR
Finish more than ten races in multi-player.

RED SHIRT RAGE CAR
Finish more than ten races in multi-player.

SHY GUY CAR
Finish more than ten races in multi-player.

GALAGA PAC JAM SONG
Unlock the Pooka car.

MUSHROOM KINGDOM II SONG
Unlock the DK Team Racing car.

SPIDER-MAN 2

ALL SPECIAL MOVES
Load the game with Spider-Man: Mysterio's Menace for Game Boy Advance in the Nintendo DS.

STAR WARS EPISODE III: REVENGE OF THE SITH

MASTER DIFFICULTY
Defeat the game.

ANAKIN'S STARFIGHTER
Beat the Anakin bot in multiplayer.

DARTH VADER'S TIE FIGHTER
Defeat Darth Vader bot in multiplayer.

GENERAL GREVIOUS'S STARFIGHTER
Defeat General Grevious bot in multiplayer.

MILLENIUM FALCON
Defeat the Solo bot in multiplayer.

SLAVE I
Defeat Fett bot in multiplayer.

X-WING
Defeat Luke bot in multiplayer.

TIGER WOODS PGA TOUR 2005

EMERALD DRAGON
Earn $1,000,000.

GREEK ISLES
Earn $1,500,000.

PARADISE COVER
Earn $2,000,000.

EA SPORTS FAVORITES
Earn $5,000,000

MEAN8TEEN
Earn $10,000,000.

FANTASY SPECIALS
Earn $15,000,000.

LEGEND COMPILATION 1
Defeat Hogan in Legend Tour.

LEGEND COMPILATION 2
Defeat Gary Player in Legend Tour.

LEGEND COMPILATION 3
Defeat Ballesteros in Legend Tour.

LEGEND COMPILATION 4
Defeat Palmer in Legend Tour.

LEGEND COMPILATION 5
Defeat Nicklaus in Legend Tour.

THE HUSTLER'S DREAM 18
Defeat The Hustler in Legend Tour.

TIGER'S DREAM 18
Defeat Tiger Woods in Legend Tour.

TOM CLANCY'S SPLINTER CELL CHAOS THEORY

UNLIMITED AMMO/GADGETS
Defeat the game.

CHARACTER SKINS
Defeat the game.

TRAUMA CENTER: UNDER THE KNIFE

X1: KYRIAKI MISSION
Defeat the game. Find the X Missions under Challenge Mode.

X2: DEFTERA MISSION
Defeat X1 : Kyriaki Mission. Find the X Missions under Challenge Mode.

X3: TRITI MISSION
Defeat X2 : Deftera Mission. Find the X Missions under Challenge Mode.

X4: TETARTI MISSION
Defeat X3 : Triti Mission. Find the X Missions under Challenge Mode.

X5: PEMPTI MISSION
Defeat X4 : Tetarti Mission. Find the X Missions under Challenge Mode.

X6: PARAKEVI MISSION
Defeat X5 : Pempti Mission. Find the X Missions under Challenge Mode.

X7: SAVATO MISSION
Defeat X6 : Parakevi Mission. Find the X Missions under Challenge Mode.

THE URBZ: SIMS IN THE CITY

CLUB XIZZLE

Once you gain access to Club Xizzle, enter with the password **"bucket."**

YU-GI-OH! NIGHTMARE TROUBADOUR

CREDITS

Unlock the Password Machine by defeating the Expert Cup. Enter the Duel Shop and select the Slot maching. Enter **00000375**.

SOUND TEST

Unlock the Password Machine by defeating the Expert Cup. Enter the Duel Shop and select the Slot maching. Enter **57300000**.

ZOO KEEPER

GEKIMUZU DIFFICULTY

Earn a high score in all 4 modes.

Here are the high scores needed for each mode:

MODE	SCORE
Zoo Keeper	200000
Tokoton 100	800000
Quest Mode	10000
Time Attack	600000

Everyone

APE ESCAPE: ON THE LOOSE
ATV OFFROAD FURY: BLAZIN' TRAILS
FIFA SOCCER
GRETZKY NHL
NBA LIVE 06
NBA STREET SHOWDOWN
NFL STREET 2 UNLEASHED
TIGER WOODS PGA TOUR
VIRTUA TENNIS: WORLD TOUR

E 10+

BURNOUT LEGENDS
HOT SHOTS GOLF: OPEN TEE

Teen

DARKSTALKERS CHRONICLE: THE CHAOS TOWER
DEATH JR.
MARVEL NEMESIS: RISE OF THE IMPERFECTS
MEDIEVIL: RESURRECTION
SPIDER-MAN 2
TONY HAWK'S UNDERGROUND 2 REMIX
TWISTED METAL: HEAD-ON
X-MEN LEGENDS II: RISE OF APOCALYPSE

PLAYSTATION® PORTABLE

Playstation® Portable
Table of Contents

APE ESCAPE: ON THE LOOSE

SNOWKIDZ RACING MINI GAME
Collect 10 Specter Coins.

SPECTER BOXING MINI GAME
Collect 20 Specter Coins.

EXTRA CHARACTERS IN SPECTER BOXING
Complete Specter Boxing.

JAKE ATTACKS MINI GAME
Collect 30 Specter Coins.

APE PING PONG MINI GAME
Collect 40 Specter Coins.

ATV OFFROAD FURY: BLAZIN' TRAILS

UNLOCK EVERYTHING...OTHER THAN THE FURY BIKE

Select Player Profile from Options. Choose Enter Cheat and enter **All Access**.

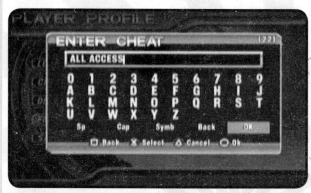

1500 CREDITS

Select Player Profile from Options. Choose Enter Cheat and enter **$moneybags$**.

ALL RIDER GEAR

Select Player Profile from Options. Choose Enter Cheat and enter **Duds**.

TIRES

Select Player Profile from Options. Choose Enter Cheat and enter **Dubs**.

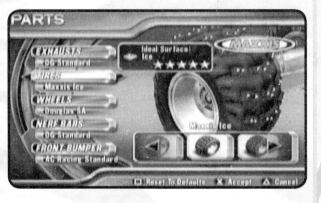

MUSIC VIDEOS

Select Player Profile from Options. Choose Enter Cheat and enter **Billboards**.

BURNOUT LEGENDS

COP RACER

Earn a Gold in all Pursuit events.

FIRETRUCK

Earn a Gold on all Crash Events.

GANGSTER BOSS

Earn Gold in all Race events.

DARKSTALKERS CHRONICLE: THE CHAOS TOWER

EX OPTIONS

At the Main menu, hold L and select Options.

MARIONETTE IN ARCADE MODE

At the character select, highlight ? and press **START** (x7), then press P or K.

OBORO BISHAMON IN ALL MODES

At the character select, highlight Bishamon, hold **START**, and press P or K.

SHADOW IN ARCADE MODE

At the character select, highlight ? and press **START** (x5), then press P or K.

DEATH JR.

CAN'T TOUCH THIS (INVINCIBILITY)

Pause the game, hold L + R and press Up, Up, Down, Down, Left, Left, Right, Right, ⬛, 🔺.

WEAPONS UPGRADED (GIVES ALL WEAPONS)

Pause the game, hold L + R and press Up, Up, Down, Down, Left, Right, Left, Right, ❌, ⬤.

AMMO REFILLED

Pause the game, hold L + R and press △, △, ✕, ✕, ■, ◉, ■, ◉, Down, Right.

UNLIMITED AMMO

Pause the game, hold L + R and press △, △, ✕, ✕, ■, ◉, ■, ◉, Right, Down.

MY HEAD FEELS FUNNY (BIG HEAD)

Pause the game, hold L + R and press △, ◉, ✕, ■, △, Up, Right, Down, Left, Up. Re-enter the code for normal head.

GIANT BLADE (BIG SCYTHE)

Pause the game, hold L + R and press △, ■, ✕, ◉, △, Up, Left, Down, Right, Up.

FREE SEEP

Pause the game, hold L + R and press Left, Left, Right, Right, Left, Right, Left, Right, ✖, ✖.

A LITTLE MORE HELP (ASSIST EXTENDER)

Pause the game, hold L + R and press Up, Up, Down, Down, ▲, ▲, ✖, ✖, ▲, ▲.

FREE WIDGET

Pause the game, hold L + R and press Right, Up, Down, Up, ▲, Up, Left, ■, ▲, Right.

GRETZKY NHL

ALL UNLOCKABLES AVAILABLE

At the Gretzky Challenge Unlockables screen, press **START**, and enter **SHOENLOC**.

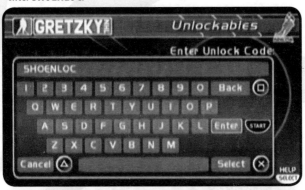

ONE GRETZKY CHALLENGE POINT

At the Gretzky Challenge Unlockables screen, press **START**, and enter **CANADIAN DOLLAR**.

BIG BOARDS CHECKING OPTION

At the Gretzky Challenge Unlockables screen, press **START**, and enter **ALL ABOARD**. You can turn this option on by selecting Unlocked Options when starting a game.

NO SKATER FATIGUE OPTION

At the Gretzky Challenge Unlockables screen, press **START**, and enter **CAFFEINATED**. You can turn this option on by selecting Unlocked Options when starting a game.

PERFECT AIM MODE OPTION

At the Gretzky Challenge Unlockables screen, press **START**, and enter **THREAD THE NEEDLE**. You can turn this option on by selecting Unlocked Options when starting a game.

PERFECT SLAP SHOTS OPTION

At the Gretzky Challenge Unlockables screen, press **START**, and enter **SLAP THAT PUCK**. You can turn this option on by selecting Unlocked Options when starting a game.

ROBOENFORCER MODEL-44

At the Gretzky Challenge Unlockables screen, press **START**, and enter **ROBO CHECKS**.

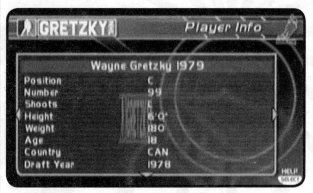

WAYNE GRETZKY - 1979 EDMONTON OILERS

At the Gretzky Challenge Unlockables screen, press **START**, and enter **UNSTOPPABLE GREATNESS**.

WAYNE GRETZKY - 1987 TEAM CANADA

At the Gretzky Challenge Unlockables screen, press **START**, and enter **GLORY DAZE**.

WAYNE GRETZKY - 1994 LOS ANGELES KINGS

At the Gretzky Challenge Unlockables screen, press **START**, and enter **WEST COAST WAYNE**.

WAYNE GRETZKY - 1999 NEW YORK RANGERS
At the Gretzky Challenge Unlockables screen, press **START**, and enter **A LEGEND ON ICE**.

ALTERNATE ANAHEIM MIGHTY DUCKS UNIFORM
At the Gretzky Challenge Unlockables screen, press **START**, and enter **FLYING VEE**.

ALTERNATE ATLANTA THRASHERS UNIFORM
At the Gretzky Challenge Unlockables screen, press **START**, and enter **THRASHED TO THE MAX**.

ALTERNATE BOSTON BRUINS UNIFORM
At the Gretzky Challenge Unlockables screen, press **START**, and enter **NOMAR STILL RULES**.

ALTERNATE BUFFALO SABERS UNIFORM
At the Gretzky Challenge Unlockables screen, press **START**, and enter **IN THE SNOW BELT**.

ALTERNATE CALGARY FLAMES UNIFORM
At the Gretzky Challenge Unlockables screen, press **START**, and enter **THREE ALARM BLAZE**.

ALTERNATE CHICAGO BLACKHAWKS UNIFORM
At the Gretzky Challenge Unlockables screen, press **START**, and enter **WINDY CITY**.

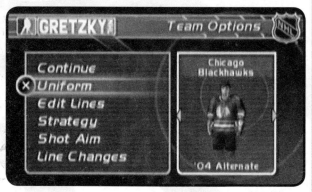

ALTERNATE COLORADO AVALANCHE UNIFORM
At the Gretzky Challenge Unlockables screen, press **START**, and enter **SNOW DRIFTS**.

ALTERNATE COLUMBUS BLUE JACKETS UNIFORM

At the Gretzky Challenge Unlockables screen, press **START**, and enter **BLUE SHOES**.

ALTERNATE DALLAS STARS UNIFORM

At the Gretzky Challenge Unlockables screen, press **START**, and enter **HOCKEY IN TEXAS**.

ALTERNATE EDMONTON OILERS UNIFORM

At the Gretzky Challenge Unlockables screen, press **START**, and enter **PUMPIN OIL**.

ALTERNATE FLORIDA PANTHERS UNIFORM

At the Gretzky Challenge Unlockables screen, press **START**, and enter **SOUTH BEACH**.

ALTERNATE LOS ANGELES KINGS UNIFORM

At the Gretzky Challenge Unlockables screen, press **START**, and enter **IT IS GOOD TO BE THE KING**.

ALTERNATE MINNESOTA WILD UNIFORM

At the Gretzky Challenge Unlockables screen, press **START**, and enter **COLD AS HECK**.

ALTERNATE NASHVILLE PREDATORS UNIFORM

At the Gretzky Challenge Unlockables screen, press **START**, and enter **ALIEN VS NASHVILLE**.

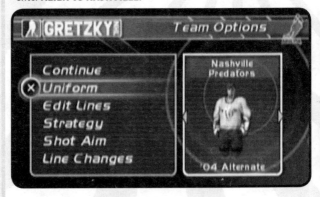

ALTERNATE NEW YORK ISLANDERS UNIFORM

At the Gretzky Challenge Unlockables screen, press **START**, and enter **LAWNG ISLAND**.

ALTERNATE NEW YORK RANGERS UNIFORM
At the Gretzky Challenge Unlockables screen, press **START**, and enter **GREAT WHITE WAY**.

ALTERNATE OTTAWA SENATORS UNIFORM
At the Gretzky Challenge Unlockables screen, press **START**, and enter **MAJORITY RULE**.

ALTERNATE PHILADELPHIA FLYERS UNIFORM
At the Gretzky Challenge Unlockables screen, press **START**, and enter **FANATICAL**.

ALTERNATE SAN JOSE SHARKS UNIFORM
At the Gretzky Challenge Unlockables screen, press **START**, and enter **GET A BIGGER BOAT**.

ALTERNATE TORONTO MAPLE LEAFS UNIFORM
At the Gretzky Challenge Unlockables screen, press **START**, and enter **HEY TERRANCE**.

ALTERNATE VANCOUVER CANUCKS UNIFORM
At the Gretzky Challenge Unlockables screen, press **START**, and enter **WEST COAST EH**.

1910 MONTREAL CANADIENS UNIFORM
At the Gretzky Challenge Unlockables screen, press **START**, and enter **THE HABS**.

1924 MONTREAL CANADIENS UNIFORM
At the Gretzky Challenge Unlockables screen, press **START**, and enter **LE HABITANT**.

1927 DETROIT RED WINGS UNIFORM
At the Gretzky Challenge Unlockables screen, press **START**, and enter **BEEP BEEP**.

1928 BOSTON BRUINS UNIFORM
At the Gretzky Challenge Unlockables screen, press **START**, and enter **WICKED HAAAAAHD**.

1929 OTTAWA SENATORS UNIFORM
At the Gretzky Challenge Unlockables screen, press **START**, and enter **THE SENANATOR**.

1930 TORONTO MAPLE LEAFS UNIFORM
At the Gretzky Challenge Unlockables screen, press **START**, and enter **NORTH OF THE BORDER**.

1967 LOS ANGELES KINGS AWAY UNIFORM
At the Gretzky Challenge Unlockables screen, press **START**, and enter **VOLLEY DOLLY**.

1967 PHILADELPHIA FLYERS AWAY UNIFORM
At the Gretzky Challenge Unlockables screen, press **START**, and enter **CHEESESTEAK**.

1967 PITTSBURGH PENGUINS AWAY UNIFORM
At the Gretzky Challenge Unlockables screen, press **START**, and enter **POPPIN TALK**.

1970 MINNESOTA NORTH STARS UNIFORM
At the Gretzky Challenge Unlockables screen, press **START**, and enter **TWIN STARS**.

1975 KANSAS CITY SCOUTS UNIFORM
At the Gretzky Challenge Unlockables screen, press **START**, and enter **YOU LITTLE DEVIL**.

1976 NEW YORK RANGERS AWAY UNIFORM
At the Gretzky Challenge Unlockables screen, press **START**, and enter **NEW YORK NEW YORK**.

1977 CALGARY FLAMES AWAY UNIFORM
At the Gretzky Challenge Unlockables screen, press **START**, and enter **FLAME ON**.

1977 COLORADO ROCKIES UNIFORM
At the Gretzky Challenge Unlockables screen, press **START**, and enter **DEVIL MADE ME DO IT**.

1977 VANCOUVER CANUCKS HOME UNIFORM
At the Gretzky Challenge Unlockables screen, press **START**, and enter **GREAT WHITE NORTH**.

1977 WASHINGTON CAPITALS AWAY UNIFORM
At the Gretzky Challenge Unlockables screen, press **START**, and enter **CONGRESSIONAL WISDOM**.

1978 NEW YORK ISLANDERS AWAY UNIFORM
At the Gretzky Challenge Unlockables screen, press **START**, and enter **ORDWAY MADE ME DO IT**.

1979 EDMONTON OILERS AWAY UNIFORM
At the Gretzky Challenge Unlockables screen, press **START**, and enter **A SCARY SIGHT TO THE HOME CROWD**.

1979 EDMONTON OILERS HOME UNIFORM
At the Gretzky Challenge Unlockables screen, press **START**, and enter **THREADS OF CHAMPS**.

1979 ST. LOUIS BLUES AWAY UNIFORM
At the Gretzky Challenge Unlockables screen, press **START**, and enter **A BLUE NOTE**.

1979 ST. LOUIS BLUES HOME UNIFORM
At the Gretzky Challenge Unlockables screen, press **START**, and enter **MARDI GRAS**.

1980 QUEBEC NORDIQUES UNIFORM
At the Gretzky Challenge Unlockables screen, press **START**, and enter **FRENCH FOR CANADIAN**.

1983 EDMONTON OILERS AWAY UNIFORM
At the Gretzky Challenge Unlockables screen, press **START**, and enter **ALL HAIL WAYNE**.

1988 PITTSBURGH PENGUINS AWAY UNIFORM

At the Gretzky Challenge Unlockables screen, press **START**, and enter **STEEL TOWN**.

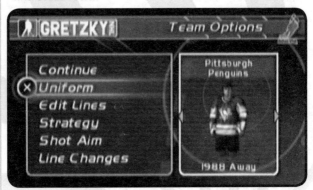

1989 LOS ANGELES KINGS AWAY UNIFORM

At the Gretzky Challenge Unlockables screen, press **START**, and enter **KING GRETZKY**.

1989 LOS ANGELES KINGS HOME UNIFORM

At the Gretzky Challenge Unlockables screen, press **START**, and enter **KING WAYNE**.

1990 WINNIPEG JETS AWAY UNIFORM

At the Gretzky Challenge Unlockables screen, press **START**, and enter **PORTAGE AND MAIN**.

1990 WINNIPEG JETS HOME UNIFORM

At the Gretzky Challenge Unlockables screen, press **START**, and enter **MIDDLE OF CANADA**.

1993 SAN JOSE SHARKS AWAY UNIFORM

At the Gretzky Challenge Unlockables screen, press **START**, and enter **SHARK BAIT**.

1995 ST. LOUIS BLUES AWAY UNIFORM

At the Gretzky Challenge Unlockables screen, press **START**, and enter **VINTAGE BLUES**.

1999 NEW YORK RANGERS HOME UNIFORM

At the Gretzky Challenge Unlockables screen, press **START**, and enter **UPPER WEST SIDE**.

HOT SHOTS GOLF: OPEN TEE

EASY DIFFICULTY FOR CHALLENGE MODE
Lose two matches or tournaments in a row. This can be changed in the Options.

AUTUMN PAGODA COURSE
Reach Beginner level in Challenge Mode.

GOLDEN DESERT COURSE
Reach Senior level in Challenge Mode.

OLIVE COAST COURSE
Reach Mid-Rank level in Challenge Mode.

5TH LOYALTY HEART
Defeat the character with a Super Win to get the 5th Loyalty Heart.

MANUAL REPLAY MODE
Reach Senior level in Challenge Mode.

MARVEL NEMESIS: RISE OF THE IMPERFECTS

BRIGADE
Finish story mode with the Thing.

IRON MAN
Finish story mode with Johnny Ohm.

SPIDER-MAN
Finish story mode with Venom.

VENOM
Finish story mode with Iron Man.

MEDIEVIL: RESURRECTION

INVINCIBILITY AND ALL WEAPONS
Pause the game, hold R and press Down, Up, ■, ▲, ▲, ●, Down, Up, ■, ▲. Pause the game to access the Cheat menu.

NBA LIVE 06

1960'S ALL-STAR TEAM
Earn all golds in Tier 1 of Superstar Challenge.

1970'S ALL-STAR TEAM
Earn all golds in Tier 2 of Superstar Challenge.

1980'S ALL-STAR TEAM
Earn all golds in Tier 3 of Superstar Challenge.

1990'S ALL-STAR TEAM
Earn all golds in Tier 4 of Superstar Challenge.

ATLANTIC DIVISION VINTAGE JERSEYS
Earn silver in Tier 1 of Superstar Challenge.

NORTHWEST DIVISION VINTAGE JERSEYS
Earn silver in Tier 2 of Superstar Challenge.

NBA STREET SHOWDOWN

UNLIMITED TURBO
During a game, hold L + R and enter ■, ■, ▲, ▲.

NFL STREET 2 UNLEASHED

Select Cheats and Codes from the Options and enter the following codes.

AFC EAST ALL STARS
Enter **EAASFSCT** as a code.

AFC NORTH ALL STARS
Enter **NAOFRCTH** as a code.

AFC SOUTH ALL STARS
Enter **SAOFUCTH** as a code.

AFC WEST ALL STARS
Enter **WAEFSCT** as a code.

NFC EAST ALL STARS
Enter **NNOFRCTH** as a code.

NFC NORTH ALL-STARS
Enter **NNAS66784** as a code.

NFC SOUTH ALL STARS
Enter **SNOFUCTH** as a code.

NFC WEST ALL STARS
Enter **ENASFSCT** as a code.

REEBOK TEAM
Enter **Reebok** as a code.

TEAM XZIBIT
Enter **TeamXzibit** as a code.

EA FIELD
Enter **EAField** as a code.

GRIDIRON FIELD
Enter **GRIDIRONPRK** as a code.

HUGE PLAYERS
Enter **BIGSmash** as a code.

BIG BALL
Enter **BIGPig** as a code.

MAX CATCH IN QUICK GAME
Enter **MagnetHands** as a code.

MAX SPEED IN QUICK GAME
Enter **GottaBdshoes** as a code.

MAX TACKLING IN QUICK GAME
Enter **BlastTackle** as a code.

DIFFICULT TO JUMP
Enter **CementShoes** as a code.

10X GAMEBREAKER
Enter **XxGBCraZ** as a code.

1X GAMEBREAKER
Enter **IIxGBCraZ** as a code.

NO FUMBLE MODE IN QUICK GAME
Enter **GlueHands** as a code.

FUMBLE MODE IN QUICK GAME
Enter **GreasedPig** as a code.

UNLIMITED TURBO IN QUICK GAME
Enter **NozBoost** as a code.

NO FIRST DOWNS
Enter **NoChains** as a code.

SPIDER-MAN 2

LEVEL WARP
Select Specials from the main menu. Choose Cheats and enter **WARPULON**.

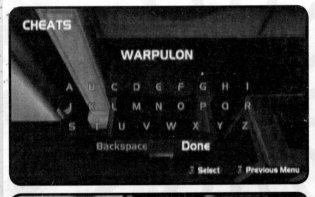

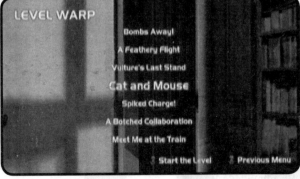

ALL MOVES

Select Specials from the main menu. Choose Cheats and enter **MYHERO**.

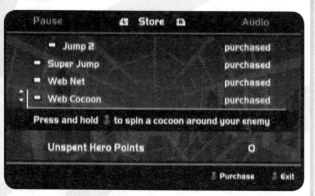

ALL MOVIES

Select Specials from the main menu. Choose Cheats and enter **POPPYCORN**.

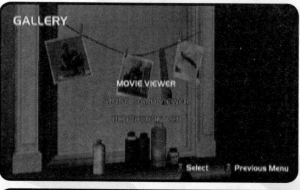

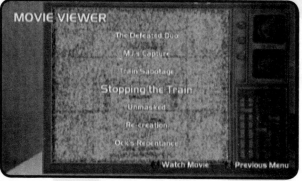

INFINITE HEALTH
Select Specials from the main menu. Choose Cheats and enter **NERGETS**.

INFINITE WEBBING
Select Specials from the main menu. Choose Cheats and enter **FILLMEUP**.

TIGER WOODS PGA TOUR

EMERALD DRAGON
Earn $1,000,000.

GREEK ISLES
Earn $1,500,000.

PARADISE COVER
Earn $2,000,000.

EA SPORTS FAVORITES
Earn $5,000,000

MEAN8TEEN
Earn $10,000,000.

FANTASY SPECIALS
Earn $15,000,000.

THE HUSTLER'S DREAM 18
Defeat The Hustler in Legend Tour.

TIGER'S DREAM 18
Defeat Tiger Woods in Legend Tour.

TONY HAWK'S UNDERGROUND 2 REMIX

PERFECT RAIL BALANCE
Select Cheat Codes from the Game Options and enter tightrope.

THPS1 TONY HAWK
Select Cheat Codes from the Game Options and enter birdman.

TWISTED METAL: HEAD-ON

These codes will not work for Multiplayer or Online modes.

HEALTH RECHARGED
Hold L + R and press ▲, ✕, ■, ●.

INFINITE AMMO
Hold L + R and press ▲, ▲, Down, Down, Left.

INVULNERABLE
Hold L + R and press Right, Left, Down, Up.

INFINITE WEAPONS
Hold L + R and press ▲, ▲, Down, Down.

KILLER WEAPONS
Hold L + R and press ✕, ✕, Up, Up.

MEGA GUNS
Hold L + R and press ✕, ▲, ✕, ▲.

VIRTUA TENNIS: WORLD TOUR

KING & QUEEN
At the Main menu, hold L and press Up, Down, Up, Down,
■, ▲, ■.

ALL RACQUETS AND CLOTHING
At the Main menu, hold L and press Right, Left, Right, Right,
Up, Up, Up.

ALL STADIUMS
At the Main menu, hold L and press Up, Down, Left, Right,
■, ■, ■.

BEGIN WORLD TOUR WITH $1,000,000

At the Main menu, hold L and press Up, Down, Left, Down,
🔵, 🔺, 🔺.

$2000 A WEEK IN WORLD TOUR

At the Main menu, hold L and press Up, Down, Right, Down,
🔵, ⬛, 🔺.

SEPIA MODE

At the Main menu, hold L and press Up, Down, Left, Right,
Left, Left, Left.

X-MEN LEGENDS II:
RISE OF APOCALYPSE

ALL COMIC BOOKS

At the review computer, press Right, Left, Left, Right, Up, Up, Right,
START.

ALL CINEMATICS

At the review computer, press Left, Right, Right, Left, Down, Down,
Left, **START**.